DIABETIC AIR FRYER COOKBOOK for BEGINNERS

1200 DAYS OF DELICIOUS, EASY & HEALTHY RECIPES FOR PRE-DIABETES, NEWLY DIAGNOSED AND TYPE 1-2 DIABETES FULL NUTRITIONAL FACTS AND 30-DAY MEAL PLAN

Ivory Holland

Copyright © 2024 by Ivory Holland

All rights reserved. No part of this publication may be reproduced, distributed, or transmitted in any form or by any means without the publisher's prior written permission.

Disclaimer:
The information and recipes in this cookbook are for educational and informational purposes only. They are not a substitute for professional medical advice, diagnosis, or treatment. Always seek the advice of your physician or other qualified health provider with any questions you may have regarding a medical condition. The author and publisher disclaim responsibility for any adverse effects resulting directly or indirectly from using the information and recipes in this book

TABLE OF CONTENTS

INTRODUCTION — 6

- WHAT IS DIABETES? — 6
- CAUSES OF DIABETES — 7
- WHAT ARE THE MAIN RISK FACTORS FOR GETTING DIABETES? — 7
- WHAT SYMPTOMS SHOULD BE ALARMING? — 7
- PREVENTION OF DIABETES — 8
- BASICS OF NUTRITION THERAPY — 8
- FOOD TO EMBRACE — 8
- FOOD TO AVOID — 9
- WHY IS AIR FRYER A BENEFIT FOR DIABETIC RECIPES? — 9

GETTING TO KNOW YOUR AIR FRYER — 10

- BASICS ABOUT AIR FRYER — 10
- TIPS AND TRICKS TO USE AN AIR FRYER — 10

BREAKFAST — 11

- VEGETABLE & EGG MUFFINS — 12
- CINNAMON-SPICED ZUCCHINI BREAD SLICES — 12
- SMOKED SALMON AND AVOCADO TOAST — 13
- CHEESY SPINACH AIR FRYER OMELETTE — 13
- AVOCADO EGG BOATS — 14
- ALMOND FLOUR CINNAMON MUFFINS — 14
- LOW-CARB BREAKFAST BURRITOS — 15
- PROTEIN-PACKED QUINOA BREAKFAST BOWL — 15
- COCONUT FLOUR PUMPKIN PANCAKES — 16
- SOUTHWEST BLACK BEAN AND SWEET POTATO BREAKFAST BOWL — 16
- ASPARAGUS AND MUSHROOM SCRAMBLE — 17
- STUFFED BELL PEPPERS WITH EGGS AND TURKEY SAUSAGE — 17
- CHICKPEA PANCAKES WITH HERBS — 18
- LOW-SUGAR APPLE FRITTERS — 18
- CHICKPEA AVOCADO TOAST — 19
- BERRY CHIA SEED BREAKFAST BARS — 19
- CAULIFLOWER HASH BROWNS — 20
- VEGETABLE AND CHEESE FRITTATA — 20
- ALMOND FLOUR BANANA BREAD SLICES — 21
- ZUCCHINI AND FETA FRITTERS — 21
- BREAKFAST PIZZA ON CAULIFLOWER CRUST — 22
- PEANUT BUTTER AND JELLY PROTEIN BARS — 22
- COCONUT FLOUR BLUEBERRY MUFFINS — 23
- EGG AND CHEESE STUFFED TOMATOES — 23
- ZUCCHINI AND CARROT MORNING GLORY MUFFINS — 24
- BREAKFAST BURRITO BOWL — 24

BLUEBERRY LEMON SCONES	25
BREAKFAST SWEET POTATO BOATS	25
GREEK-STYLE SPINACH AND OLIVE BREAKFAST MUFFINS	26
PECAN PIE GRANOLA BARS	26

SALADS   27

CRUNCHY GREENS SALAD WITH GRILLED CHICKEN AND HERBS	28
MEDITERRANEAN TUNA SALAD WITH FRESH HERBS	28
SPINACH & STRAWBERRY SALAD WITH BALSAMIC VINAIGRETTE	29
LOW-CARB CAESAR SALAD WITH SHRIMP	29
GRILLED SALMON KALE SALAD WITH LEMON DRESSING	30
ASIAN STYLE BROCCOLI SLAW WITH CRUNCHY TOFU	30
FRESH GARDEN VEGETABLE QUINOA BOWL	31
MARINATED ARTICHOKE HEARTS AND SHRIMP PASTA-SALAD	31
SUMMER BERRY ALMOND SPINACH SALAD	32
ROASTED PUMPKIN AND ARUGULA SUPERFOOD BOWL	32
GRILLED CHICKEN AND AVOCADO SALAD	33
WARM SALMON NIÇOISE SALAD	33
SPICY SWEET POTATO AND BLACK BEAN SALAD	34
ASPARAGUS AND GOAT CHEESE SALAD	34
WARM MEDITERRANEAN VEGETABLE SALAD	35
CRISPY AIR-FRIED CHICKPEA SALAD	35
WARM MUSHROOM AND SPINACH SALAD	36
PEAR AND WALNUT WINTER SALAD	36
BEETROOT AND FETA SALAD	37
WARM HALLOUMI AND TOMATO SALAD	37

SIDES   38

AIR-FRIED GREEN BEANS ALMONDINE	39
LEMON-PEPPER ASPARAGUS SPEARS	39
CAULIFLOWER 'MAC' AND CHEESE	40
CHICKEN BRUSCHETTA	40
SPICY OKRA WITH COOL YOGURT DIP	41
CRISPY BRUSSELS SPROUTS WITH BALSAMIC GLAZE	41
GARLIC & ROSEMARY ROASTED TURNIPS	42
CAULIFLOWER RICE PILAF WITH CARROTS AND PEAS	42
SESAME GINGER BROCCOLI STIR-FRY	43
ITALIAN HERB ROASTED BELL PEPPERS	43
ITALIAN BAKED EGGPLANT STICKS WITH MARINARA DIP	44
SWEET & SAVORY BUTTERNUT SQUASH WEDGES	44
FRESH HERBS AND LEMON GREEN BEANS	45
MEDITERRANEAN SPICED AIR FRYER CHICKPEAS	45
STUFFED MUSHROOM CAPS WITH SPINACH AND RICOTTA	46
GARLIC-PARMESAN AIR FRYER BRUSSELS SPROUTS	46

SOUPS   47

CREAMY BROCCOLI SOUP WITH AIR-FRYER CROUTONS	48
LOW-CARB TOMATO BASIL SOUP WITH PARMESAN CRISPS	48
SPICY CHICKEN & VEGGIE SOUP WITH TORTILLA STRIPS	49
VEGETABLE BARLEY SOUP	49
CAULIFLOWER & CHEDDAR CHEESE SOUP	50
ROASTED RED PEPPER GAZPACHO	50
ROASTED PUMPKIN BISQUE WITH GREEK YOGURT SWIRL	51
CREAMY MUSHROOM SOUP WITH THYME	51
CHICKEN ZOODLE PRO	52
HEARTY TURKEY AND BEAN CHILI SOUP	52
CLASSIC MINESTRONE MADE LOW-CARB	53
CHICKEN MEATBALL ITALIAN WEDDING SOUP	53

TURKEY 54

TURKEY & VEGETABLE STIR FRY	55
LOW-CARB TURKEY STUFFED BELL PEPPERS	55
ZESTY LEMON-GARLIC TURKEY BREAST	56
CRISPY TURKEY TACOS WITH AVOCADO CREMA	56
TURKEY TENDERLOIN WITH ROASTED VEGETABLES	57
SPICY GROUND TURKEY LETTUCE WRAPS	57
ROSEMARY & GARLIC INFUSED TURKEY LEGS	58
TURKEY MEATBALL SOUP WITH SPIRALIZED VEGGIES	58
BALSAMIC GLAZED BRUSSELS SPROUTS & GROUND TURKEY	59
STUFFED PORTOBELLO MUSHROOMS WITH GROUND TURKEY & FETA CHEESE	59
THANKSGIVING-STYLE SLICED TURKEY BREAST	60
TURKEY ZUCCHINI BOATS WITH MOZZARELLA TOPPING	60
BBQ BASTED MINI-TURKEY MEATLOAVES	61
ASIAN-INSPIRED GROUND TURKEY WRAPS	61
HEARTY TURKEY SAUSAGE CASSEROLE	62
PARMESAN-CRUSTED TURKEY TENDERS	62
SESAME-GINGER TURKEY MEATBALLS	63
BUFFALO-STYLE TURKEY DRUMSTICKS	63
GREEK-STYLE TURKEY BURGERS WITH TZATZIKI	64
TERIYAKI TURKEY SKEWERS WITH PINEAPPLE	64

CHICKEN 65

CHICKEN BREAST WITH STEAMED BROCCOLI	66
SAVORY GARLIC & HERB CHICKEN DRUMSTICKS	66
HEALTHY CHICKEN CORDON BLEU	67
BUFFALO CHICKEN WINGS WITH CELERY STICKS	67
CRISPY SESAME GINGER CHICKEN THIGHS	68
MEDITERRANEAN GREEK SALAD WITH GRILLED CHICKEN	68
ROSEMARY GARLIC ROASTED WHOLE CHICKEN	69
TERIYAKI GLAZED DRUMSTICKS	69
MEXICAN FIESTA STUFFED ORGANIC CHICKEN BREAST	70
COCONUT CURRY CRUSTED CHICKEN TENDERS	70
PARMESAN CRUSTED ORGANIC CHICKEN FILLETS	71
CAPRESE STYLE STUFFED GRILLED-CHICKEN	71

BBQ Pulled Grilled-Chicken Lettuce Wraps	72
Chicken Piccata with Capers	72
Chicken Bruschetta (No-Bread Version)	73
Chicken Satay with Peanut Sauce	73
Chicken and Zucchini Meatballs	74
Chicken Tenders with Almond Flour Coating	74
Curry-Spiced Chicken Thighs	75
Greek Yogurt Marinated Chicken Skewers	75

BEEF 76

Beef and Broccoli Stir-fry	77
Stuffed Bell Peppers with Ground Beef	77
Marinated Flank Steak with Grilled Veggies	78
Garlic-Herb Crusted Roast Beef	78
Ground Beef Lettuce Wraps with Avocado Salsa	79
Pepper-Steak Skewers	79
Balsamic-Glazed Top Sirloin Steak with Asparagus	80
Homemade Beef Meatballs	80
Zesty Lime & Chili Flank Steak Fajitas	81
Sesame-Ginger Beef Stir-Fry	81
Cheesy Stuffed Mushrooms with Minced Beef	82
Hearty Grilled Aubergine & Ground Beef Lasagna	82

LAMB 83

Rosemary and Thyme-Infused Lamb Chops	84
Mediterranean Lamb Kebabs with Tzatziki Sauce	84
Shepherd's Pie with Cauliflower Mash	85
Cumin Spiced Lamb Skewers with Grilled Veggies	85
Greek Style Stuffed Bell Peppers with Ground Lamb	86
Moroccan-Inspired Lamb Shanks	86
Skillet-style Ground Lamb and Eggplant Moussaka	87
Herb-Crusted Rack of Lamb with Grilled Asparagus	87
Garlic & Lemongrass Leg of Lamb	88
Lamb Meatballs Stuffed with Feta Cheese	88
Spinach & Minced Lamb Stuffed Zucchini Boats	89
Middle Eastern Kofta Wraps	89
Grilled Ratatouille Salad & Marinated Lamb Cutlets	90
Spicy Lamb Tenderloin Steaks	90

PORK 91

Garlic and Herb Pork Tenderloin	92
Parmesan Crusted Pork Chops	92
Stuffed Bell Peppers with Ground Pork	93
Lean Pork Skewers with Lemon Zest	93
Stir-Fried Bok Choy and Shredded Pork	94
Sweet Mustard Glazed Ham Steaks	94

CHINESE-STYLE BARBECUED PORK RIBS	95
ROSEMARY INFUSED GRILLED BONELESS LOIN ROAST	95
APPLE CIDER MARINATED LEAN PULLED-PORK WRAPS	96
CRISPY ASIAN-INSPIRED SALT & PEPPER SPARE RIBS	96
SPICY GROUND PORK STUFFED MUSHROOM CAPS	97
PORK TENDERLOIN WITH FRESH HERBS	97
LEAN BACON-WRAPPED ASPARAGUS SKEWERS	98
SWEET & SOUR PULLED-PORK LETTUCE WRAPS	98

FISH AND SEAFOOD   99

ZESTY LEMON GARLIC AIR-FRIED SALMON FILLETS	100
SHRIMP SCAMPI WITH ZUCCHINI NOODLES	100
TERIYAKI GLAZED TUNA STEAKS	101
CHILI-LIME COD FISH TACOS WRAPPED IN LETTUCE	101
CAJUN SPICED CATFISH WITH SAUTÉED SPINACH	102
HERB-CRUSTED HADDOCK WITH STEAMED BROCCOLI	102
LEMON PEPPER SCALLOPS	103
CAJUN SHRIMP SKEWERS WITH GRILLED BELL PEPPERS	103
ASIAN-STYLE SESAME GINGER SALMON PATTIES	104
MEDITERRANEAN STUFFED CALAMARI RINGS	104
SPICY PANKO CRUSTED TILAPIA FILETS	105
FRAGRANT HALIBUT STEAKS WITH CITRUS VINAIGRETTE	105
MUSHROOM CAPS STUFFED WITH CLAMS	106
COCONUT SHRIMP WITH AVOCADO DIP	106

DESSERTS   107

CINNAMON AND ALMOND BISCOTTI	108
COCONUT AND BLUEBERRY CHEESECAKE BITES	108
DARK CHOCOLATE DIPPED STRAWBERRIES	109
VANILLA BEAN CUSTARD STUFFED PEACHES	109
ALMOND JOY KETO COOKIES	110
PEANUT BUTTER BANANA MUFFINS	110
LEMON BLUEBERRY CAKE	111
CINNAMON APPLE CHIPS WITH A TOUCH OF STEVIA	111
GLUTEN-FREE STRAWBERRY RHUBARB CRUMBLE	112
CHIA RASPBERRY JAM FILLED DOUGHNUT HOLES	112
LOW-SUGAR HAZELNUT CHOCOLATE TRUFFLES	113
BERRIES AND OATS CRUNCHY GRANOLA BARS	113
KETO AVOCADO BROWNIES	114
CREAMY GREEK YOGURT CHEESECAKE WITH MIXED BERRIES	114

30-DAY MEAL PLAN   115

RECIPE INDEX   119

Introduction

Diabetes mellitus is one of the incurable diseases. Back in the 20th century, this diagnosis was a death sentence. The only thing doctors could do was to put patients on a severe diet and thereby prolong their lives. In the 21st century, the disease affects one in 20 people, and by mid-century, almost half a billion people will be living with this diagnosis. However, there is some good news! People have learned how to control diabetes through many decades of scientific discoveries and medical advances. The progress in this field has dramatically improved diabetes treatment, often enabling individuals to enjoy a quality of life similar to that of completely healthy people.

Food is one of modern people's main pleasures and their main problem. Regular overeating and excessive caloric intake can lead to disease or prevent its treatment. For a diabetic, nutrition is not just about satisfying hunger but is an integral part of treatment on par with medication and sports. A diabetic-friendly diet is essential for managing blood sugar levels, preventing complications, supporting overall health, and improving the quality of life for people with diabetes by providing balanced nutrition that minimizes glucose spikes and reduces the body's insulin demand.

If you're reading this page, it means you've already started living a healthy lifestyle. As a chef and nutritionist with many years of experience, I will help you improve your nutrition as a person with diabetes and prepare meals from healthy ingredients packed with fiber, healthy fats, and vitamins. Diabetic Air Fryer Cookbook for Beginners includes many delicious, easy recipes that help manage blood sugar while satisfying taste buds, empowering people with diabetes to enjoy food without compromise.

What is Diabetes?

Diabetes is a condition that impairs your body's ability to process food into usable energy. It occurs when blood glucose (sugar) levels are too high. This is due to impaired absorption of sugar from the blood into the body's cells. The hormone insulin is needed for the body's cells to use sugar from food as an energy source. In people with diabetes, insulin action is reduced, and the pancreas produces too little or no insulin. Consequences: sugar stays in the blood, and blood sugar levels rise.

There are two types of diabetes: type 1, when the body does not produce enough insulin, and type 2, when the body cannot effectively use the insulin it does make.

Type 1 diabetes impacts children and young people under 30 years of age. Although Type 1 diabetes cannot be cured, recognizing it early and implementing appropriate care can help avoid dire health consequences in the future.

Type 2 diabetes is a disease of the adults. Diabetes often occurs due to excess weight and insufficient physical activity; genetic predisposition is essential as well. Therefore, if people with diabetes are members of a family, switching the whole family to a healthy lifestyle will not be superfluous.

Causes of diabetes

1. **Type 1 Diabetes:**
   - Autoimmune reaction: The body's immune system attacks insulin-producing cells in the pancreas
   - Genetic factors
   - Environmental triggers (possibly viruses)
2. **Type 2 Diabetes:**
   - Insulin resistance: Cells don't respond effectively to insulin
   - Genetics
   - Lifestyle factors: • Obesity • Lack of physical activity • Poor diet
   - Age (risk increases with age)
   - Ethnicity (some groups are at higher risk)

What are the main risk factors for getting diabetes?

- A sedentary lifestyle increases the risk of developing diabetes. During physical activity, glucose moves from the blood to the muscles and is used as an energy source. If a person does not move, glucose remains in the blood.
- Fat in the waist area. Excess pounds deposited in the waist area are often metabolic syndrome, in which the sensitivity of cells to insulin is reduced.
- Diabetes in immediate family members. If siblings or parents have diabetes, the risk of developing the disease is increased.
- Lack of sleep. In those who do not get enough sleep, the body releases stress hormones that stimulate appetite. Because of this, people who regularly sleep less than 5 or 6 hours often gain weight.
- Increased blood pressure. People with hypertension have a two times greater risk of diabetes compared to people with normal blood pressure.
- Age. Type 2 diabetes mellitus more often develops after 35-40 years of age. Women need to be especially careful: at this age, menopause begins, metabolism slows down, and weight often increases.
- Elevated glucose levels. For those in the risk group, it is critical to monitor blood glucose levels.

Having risk factors doesn't guarantee that you'll develop diabetes, but it does increase your chances. Many of these factors are modifiable through lifestyle changes.

What symptoms should be alarming?

- Thirst and dry mouth. Drinking much more than before, sometimes up to 3-5 liters daily.
- Abrupt weight loss for no reason.
- Constant fatigue, irritability, weakness, drowsiness.
- Frequent and profuse urination.
- Sudden attacks of nausea and vomiting
- Numbness in the hands and feet, a tingling sensation in the fingers.
- A feeling of hunger.
- Poor wound healing.
- Itching of the skin.
- Deterioration of vision

Prevention of diabetes

- Keep a healthy weight: lose excess weight if overweight or obese, and aim for a BMI in the healthy range
- Exercise regularly: aim for at least 120 minutes of moderate aerobic activity per week, including strength training exercises
- Eat a balanced diet: focus on whole grains, lean proteins, fruits, and vegetables; limit processed foods, sugary drinks, and excessive carbohydrates
- Control portion sizes: use smaller plates
- Quit smoking, or don't start
- Limit alcohol consumption
- Manage stress: practice relaxation techniques; get enough sleep (7-9 hours nightly)
- Regular health check-ups: monitor blood pressure, cholesterol, and blood sugar levels
- Stay hydrated: choose water over sugary drinks

Basics of nutrition therapy

- Carbohydrate management: focus on portion control; choose complex carbs over simple sugars; monitor glycemic index of foods
- Balanced meals: include protein, healthy fats, and fiber with carbs; use the plate method (1/2 non-starchy veggies, 1/4 protein, 1/4 carbs)
- Consistent meal timing: eat at regular intervals to maintain stable blood sugar
- Individualized approach: tailor plans to personal preferences, cultural background, and lifestyle
- Blood glucose monitoring: learn how different foods affect blood sugar levels
- Portion control: use measuring tools or visual guides to manage serving sizes
- Emphasis on whole foods: prioritize unprocessed foods over packaged or refined options
- Hydration: choose water and other sugar-free beverages
- Fiber intake: aim for 25-30 grams daily to aid blood sugar control
- Limit added sugars and saturated fats: read labels and choose healthier alternatives

Food to embrace

- ☺ Non-starchy vegetables: leafy greens (spinach, kale); broccoli, cauliflower; bell peppers, tomatoes, carrots, cucumber
- ☺ Whole grains: brown rice, quinoa, whole wheat bread, oatmeal
- ☺ Lean proteins: chicken, turkey, fish (especially fatty fish like salmon), eggs, tofu, tempeh
- ☺ Legumes: lentils, chickpeas, black beans, kidney beans
- ☺ Healthy fats: avocados, nuts (almonds, walnuts), seeds (chia, flax), olive oil
- ☺ Low-fat dairy: Greek yogurt, cottage cheese
- ☺ Berries: strawberries, blueberries, raspberries, blackberries
- ☺ Citrus fruits: oranges, grapefruits
- ☺ Sweet potatoes
- ☺ Green tea

Food to avoid

- ☹ Sugary beverages: soda, sweetened tea or coffee drinks, fruit juices with added sugars
- ☹ Refined carbohydrates: white bread, pasta, rice, sugary cereals
- ☹ Processed snack foods: chips, crackers made with refined flour, pretzels
- ☹ Sweets and desserts: candy, cookies, cakes, ice cream
- ☹ Fried foods: French fries, fried chicken, doughnuts
- ☹ High-fat dairy products: full-fat cheese, cream, whole milk
- ☹ Fatty meats: bacon, sausages, highly marbled cuts of beef
- ☹ Alcohol (in excess): can interfere with blood sugar control
- ☹ Trans fats: found in some processed foods and baked goods
- ☹ High-sodium foods: canned soups, processed meats, some condiments
- ☹ Large portions of dried fruit can be high in concentrated sugars
- ☹ Sweetened yogurts

Why is Air Fryer a benefit for diabetic recipes?

Air fryers benefit diabetic recipes by significantly reducing oil usage, aiding weight management and blood sugar control. The lower oil content may result in foods with a lower glycemic impact, helping maintain more stable blood sugar levels. Air fryers' shorter cooking times can preserve more nutrients in foods, enhancing the overall nutritional value of meals. These appliances offer versatility, allowing the preparation of a wide range of diabetic-friendly foods, including vegetables and lean meats. Air fryers provide a satisfying crispy texture without deep frying, meeting cravings for crispy foods more healthily. The size of the air fryer basket can assist with portion management, an essential aspect of diabetes management. The convenience and quick cooking times of air fryers make preparing healthy meals at home more accessible, encouraging cooking from scratch and avoiding processed foods. As a lower-fat cooking method, air fryers allow the enjoyment of traditionally high-fat foods more healthily. The easy cleanup associated with air fryers simplifies meal preparation, making healthy cooking more appealing. Precise temperature control in air fryers helps avoid overcooking or burning foods, ensuring optimal preparation of diabetic-friendly meals.

Getting to Know Your Air Fryer

Basics about Air Fryer

Air fryers are compact kitchen devices that cook food by circulating hot air, creating a crispy exterior with minimal oil. They offer a healthier alternative to deep frying and can fry, roast, and bake various foods. Air fryers are easy to use, with adjustable temperatures and timers, and come in different sizes. While they produce crispy results, the taste may differ slightly from traditional deep-fried foods. These versatile devices are essentially small convection ovens suitable for various cooking methods beyond frying.

Tips and Tricks to Use an Air Fryer

1) Preheat for optimal crispiness and shorter cooking times.
2) Use a light coating of oil spray for better browning and texture.
3) Refrain from overfilling the basket to ensure proper air circulation and even cooking.
4) Shake the basket or flip food halfway through for uniform crispiness.
5) Use parchment paper or foil liners for easier cleanup with messy foods.
6) Adjust cooking times for frozen foods, which usually require longer durations.
7) Experiment with different temperatures for various foods and textures.
8) Add water to the drawer when cooking fatty foods to prevent smoking.
9) Use bread crumbs or seasoned coatings for extra crunch.
10) Clean your air fryer regularly to maintain performance and prevent odors.

These tips can help you achieve the best results and maximize your air fryer's capabilities.

Breakfast

Vegetable & Egg Muffins

Prep. time: 10 **Cook time:** 12-15 **Servings:** 4

Ingredients:

- 8 large eggs
- 1/4 cup unsweetened almond milk
- 1 cup spinach, chopped
- 1/2 cup bell peppers, diced
- 1/4 cup onion, finely diced
- 1/4 cup mushrooms, chopped
- 1/4 cup cherry tomatoes, halved
- 1/4 cup shredded cheddar cheese
- 1 tsp dried basil
- 1/2 tsp garlic powder
- Salt and pepper to taste
- Cooking spray

Directions:

1. Preheat the air fryer to 300°F (150°C).
2. Whisk eggs, almond milk, basil, garlic powder, salt, and pepper.
3. Stir in vegetables and cheese.
4. Spray silicone muffin cups with cooking spray.
5. Pour egg mixture into cups, filling 3/4 full.
6. Place cups in the air fryer basket.
7. Cook for 12-15 minutes until set and lightly golden.

Serving suggestion: Serve warm. These muffins can be made and reheated for a quick, nutritious breakfast or snack.

Nutritional Information (per serving - 2 muffins): Calories: 220 | Protein: 18g | Carbohydrates: 5g | Fiber: 1g | Net Carbs: 4g | Fat: 15g (saturated: 5g) | Cholesterol: 380mg | Sodium: 300mg | Potassium: 300mg

Cinnamon-Spiced Zucchini Bread Slices

Prep. time: 15 min **Cook time:** 25 min **Servings:** 4

Ingredients:

- 2 cups almond flour
- 1 medium zucchini, grated (about 1 cup)
- 2 large eggs
- 1/4 cup unsweetened applesauce
- 2 tbsp coconut oil, melted
- 2 tbsp erythritol sweetener
- 1 tsp baking powder
- 1 tsp ground cinnamon
- 1/2 tsp vanilla extract
- 1/4 tsp salt
- 1/4 cup chopped walnuts (optional)

Directions:

1. Preheat the air fryer to 300°F (150°C).
2. In a large bowl, mix almond flour, erythritol, baking powder, cinnamon, and salt
3. Whisk eggs, applesauce, melted coconut oil, and vanilla in another bowl.
4. Combine wet and dry ingredients. Fold in grated zucchini and walnuts if using.
5. Put the air fryer basket with parchment paper. Pour batter in, spreading evenly.
6. Air fry for 20-25 minutes until a toothpick comes out clean.
7. Let cool for 10 minutes, then slice into eight pieces.

Serving suggestion: Serve warm with a dollop of Greek yogurt.

Nutritional information per serving (2 slices): Calories: 290 | Protein: 11g | Carbohydrates: 10g | Fiber: 5g | Net carbs: 5g | Fat: 24g | Cholesterol: 93mg | Sodium: 220mg | Potassium: 260mg

Smoked Salmon and Avocado Toast

Prep. time: 10 min **Cook time:** 5 min **Servings:** 4

Ingredients:

- 4 slices whole grain bread
- 8 oz smoked salmon
- 1 large ripe avocado
- 1 tbsp lemon juice
- 1/4 tsp garlic powder
- 1/4 tsp onion powder
- Salt and pepper to taste
- 2 tbsp capers, drained (optional)
- 1/4 red onion, thinly sliced (optional)

Directions:

1. Preheat the air fryer to 350°F (175°C).
2. Place bread slices in an air fryer basket. Cook for 3-4 minutes until crispy, flipping halfway through.
3. Mash avocado with lemon juice, garlic powder, onion powder, salt, and pepper.
4. Spread the avocado mixture on toasted bread.
5. Top with smoked salmon, capers, and red onion if using.

Serving suggestion: Garnish with fresh dill or a sprinkle of everything bagel seasoning.

Nutritional information per serving (1 toast): Calories: 250 | Protein: 15g | Carbohydrates: 20g | Fiber: 6g | Net carbs: 14g | Fat: 13g | Cholesterol: 10mg | Sodium: 650mg | Potassium: 400mg

Cheesy Spinach Air Fryer Omelette

Prep. time: 10 min **Cook time:** 15 min **Servings:** 4

Ingredients:

Ingredients:

- 8 large eggs
- 2 cups fresh spinach, chopped
- 1/2 cup shredded cheddar cheese
- 1/4 cup milk
- 1/4 cup diced bell peppers
- 2 tbsp chopped onions
- 1/4 tsp garlic powder
- Salt and pepper to taste
- Cooking spray

Directions:

1. Preheat the air fryer to 300°F (150°C).
2. Whisk eggs, milk, garlic powder, salt, and pepper in a large bowl.
3. Stir in spinach, cheese, bell peppers, and onions.
4. Lightly coat the air fryer basket with cooking spray.
5. Pour the egg mixture into the basket.
6. Cook for 12-15 minutes until set and lightly golden on top.
7. Carefully remove and slice into quarters.

Serving suggestion: Serve with a side of cherry tomatoes or a small mixed green salad.

Nutritional information per serving: Calories: 220 | Protein: 17g | Carbohydrates: 3g | Fiber: 1g | Net carbs: 2g | Fat: 16g | Cholesterol: 385mg | Sodium: 300mg | Potassium: 300mg

Avocado Egg Boats

Prep. time: 10 min | **Cook time:** 12 min | **Servings:** 4

Ingredients:

- 2 large ripe avocados
- 4 large eggs
- 2 tbsp crumbled feta cheese
- 2 tbsp chopped fresh chives
- 1/4 tsp smoked paprika
- Salt and pepper to taste
- Cooking spray

Directions:

1. Preheat the air fryer to 350°F (175°C).
2. Cut avocados in half and remove pits. Scoop out a bit more flesh to make room for the egg.
3. Lightly spray the air fryer basket with cooking spray.
4. Place avocado halves in the basket and cut side up.
5. Carefully crack an egg into each avocado half.
6. Air fry for 10-12 minutes until egg whites are set, but yolks are still runny.
7. Sprinkle with feta, chives, smoked paprika, salt, and pepper.

Serving suggestion: Serve with a side of mixed greens or sliced tomatoes.

Nutritional information per serving (1 avocado half): Calories: 240 | Protein: 10g | Carbohydrates: 9g | Fiber: 7g | Net carbs: 2g | Fat: 20g | Cholesterol: 190mg | Sodium: 180mg | Potassium: 500mg

Almond Flour Cinnamon Muffins

Prep. time: 15 min | **Cook time:** 12 min | **Servings:** 4

Ingredients:

- 2 cups almond flour
- 1/4 cup erythritol
- 2 tsp baking powder
- 2 tsp ground cinnamon
- 1/4 tsp salt
- 4 large eggs
- 1/4 cup unsweetened almond milk
- 2 tbsp coconut oil, melted
- 1 tsp vanilla extract
- 1/4 cup chopped walnuts (optional)

Directions:

Instructions:

1. Preheat the air fryer to 300°F (150°C).
2. Mix almond flour, erythritol, baking powder, cinnamon, and salt in a bowl.
3. Whisk eggs, almond milk, melted coconut oil, and vanilla in another bowl.
4. Combine wet and dry ingredients. Fold in walnuts if using.
5. Line the air fryer basket with silicone muffin cups or parchment paper liners.
6. Fill each cup 2/3 full with batter.
7. Air fry for 12-15 minutes until a toothpick comes out clean.
8. Let cool for 5 minutes before removing from cups.

Serving suggestion: Enjoy warm or room temperature with a dollop of Greek yogurt.

Nutritional information per serving (2 muffins): Calories: 340 | Protein: 13g | Carbohydrates: 9g | Fiber: 5g | Net carbs: 4g | Fat: 29g | Cholesterol: 185mg | Sodium: 330mg | Potassium: 230mg

Low-Carb Breakfast Burritos

🥣 **Prep. time:** 15 min 🕐 **Cook time:** 10min 🍴 **Servings:** 4

Ingredients:

- 4 large eggs
- 1/4 cup unsweetened almond milk
- 1 cup spinach, chopped
- 1/4 cup bell peppers, diced
- 1/4 cup onions, diced
- 1/2 cup cheddar cheese, shredded
- 4 low-carb tortillas
- 1/4 tsp garlic powder
- Salt and pepper to taste
- Cooking spray

Directions:

1. Preheat the air fryer to 350°F (175°C).
2. Whisk eggs, almond milk, garlic powder, salt, and pepper in a bowl.
3. Spray a pan with cooking spray. Scramble egg mixture with vegetables over medium heat until just set.
4. Divide egg mixture and cheese among tortillas. Roll into burritos.
5. Lightly spray air fryer basket and burritos with cooking spray.
6. Place burritos seam-side down in the basket.
7. Air fry for 5-7 minutes, flipping halfway, until golden and crispy.

Serving suggestion: Serve with a side of salsa or guacamole.

Nutritional information per serving (1 burrito): Calories: 280 | Protein: 18g | Carbohydrates: 12g (varies with tortilla brand) | Fiber: 7g | Net carbs: 5g | Fat: 18g | Cholesterol: 205mg | Sodium: 450mg | Potassium: 250mg

Protein-Packed Quinoa Breakfast Bowl

🥣 **Prep. time:** 15 min 🕐 **Cook time:** 20 min 🍴 **Servings:** 4

Ingredients:

- 1 cup quinoa, rinsed
- 2 cups water
- 1 cup mixed vegetables (bell peppers, zucchini, onions)
- 1 cup cherry tomatoes, halved
- 4 large eggs
- 1/4 cup crumbled feta cheese
- 2 tbsp olive oil
- 1 tsp dried oregano
- Salt and pepper to taste

Directions:

1. Cook quinoa with water according to package instructions. Set aside.
2. Preheat the air fryer to 380°F (190°C).
3. Toss vegetables and tomatoes with 1 tbsp olive oil, oregano, salt, and pepper.
4. Air fry vegetables for 10 minutes, shaking the basket halfway through.
5. Divide quinoa among 4 bowls. Top with air-fried vegetables.
6. Make 4 wells in the vegetables. Crack an egg into each well.
7. Air fry for 5-6 minutes until egg whites are set, but yolks are still runny.
8. Sprinkle feta cheese over the bowls.

Serving suggestion: Drizzle with olive oil and add fresh herbs if desired.

Nutritional information per serving: Calories: 340 | Protein: 16g | Carbohydrates: 38g | Fiber: 6g | Net carbs: 32g | Fat: 15g | Cholesterol: 190mg | Sodium: 280mg | Potassium: 520mg

Coconut Flour Pumpkin Pancakes

Prep. time: 10 min **Cook time:** 15 min **Servings:** 4

Ingredients:

- 1/2 cup coconut flour
- 1/2 cup pumpkin puree
- 4 large eggs
- 1/4 cup unsweetened almond milk
- 2 tbsp erythritol
- 1 tsp baking powder
- 1 tsp pumpkin pie spice
- 1/4 tsp salt
- Cooking spray

Directions:

1. Whisk together coconut flour, erythritol, baking powder, pumpkin pie spice, and salt in a bowl.
2. Mix pumpkin puree, eggs, and almond milk in another bowl.
3. Combine wet and dry ingredients, stirring until smooth.
4. Preheat the air fryer to 350°F (175°C).
5. Line the air fryer basket with parchment paper and lightly spray it with cooking spray.
6. Drop batter by 2 tablespoons onto the parchment paper, leaving space between each.
7. Air fry for 5-6 minutes, then carefully flip and cook for another 2-3 minutes.
8. Repeat with the remaining batter.

Serving suggestion: Top with a dollop of Greek yogurt and a sprinkle of chopped nuts.

Nutritional information (3 small pancakes): Calories: 180 | Protein: 10g | Carbohydrates: 12g | Fiber: 7g | Net carbs: 5g | Fat: 11g | Cholesterol: 185mg | Sodium: 300mg | Potassium: 200mg

Southwest Black Bean and Sweet Potato

Prep. time: 15 min **Cook time:** 20 min **Servings:** 4

Ingredients:

- 2 medium sweet potatoes, diced
- 1 can (15 oz) black beans, drained and rinsed
- 1 red bell pepper, diced
- 1 small red onion, diced
- 2 tbsp olive oil
- 1 tsp ground cumin
- 1 tsp smoked paprika
- 1/2 tsp chili powder
- Salt and pepper to taste
- 4 large eggs
- 1/4 cup cilantro, chopped
- 1 avocado, sliced

Directions:

1. Preheat the air fryer to 380°F (190°C).
2. In a bowl, toss sweet potatoes, bell pepper, and onion with 1 tbsp olive oil, cumin, paprika, chili powder, salt, and pepper.
3. Air fry for 15 minutes, shaking basket every 5 minutes.
4. Add black beans to the basket, shake, and air fry for 5 more minutes.
5. Divide mixture among 4 bowls.
6. Crack eggs into small ramekins or silicone cups.
7. Place cups in an air fryer basket and cook at 350°F (175°C) for 5-6 minutes for set whites and runny yolks.
8. Top each bowl with an egg, sliced avocado, and cilantro.

Serving suggestion: Add a dollop of Greek yogurt or a sprinkle of low-fat cheese if desired.

Nutritional information per serving: Calories: 380 | Protein: 17g | Carbohydrates: 45g | Fiber: 13g | Net carbs: 32g | Fat: 18g | Cholesterol: 185mg | Sodium: 300mg | Potassium: 850mg

Asparagus and Mushroom Scramble

Prep. time: 10 min   **Cook time:** 15 min   **Servings:** 4

Ingredients:

- 8 large eggs
- 1 bunch asparagus, trimmed and cut into 1-inch pieces
- 8 oz mushrooms, sliced
- 1/4 cup unsweetened almond milk
- 2 tbsp olive oil
- 1/4 cup grated Parmesan cheese
- 1 tsp dried thyme
- Salt and pepper to taste

Directions:

1. Preheat the air fryer to 375°F (190°C).
2. Toss asparagus and mushrooms with 1 tbsp olive oil, thyme, salt, and pepper.
3. Air fry vegetables for 8-10 minutes, shaking basket halfway through.
4. Whisk eggs, almond milk, salt, and pepper in a bowl.
5. Pour egg mixture over vegetables in the air fryer basket.
6. Cook for 5-7 minutes, stirring gently every 2 minutes, until eggs are set.
7. Sprinkle Parmesan cheese over the scramble and cook for 1 more minute.

Serving suggestion: Garnish with fresh herbs and serve with cherry tomatoes.

Nutritional information per serving: Calories: 260 | Protein: 19g | Carbohydrates: 6g | Fiber: 2g | Net carbs: 4g | Fat: 19g | Cholesterol: 375mg | Sodium: 280mg | Potassium: 400mg

Stuffed Bell Peppers with Eggs and Turkey Sausage

Prep. time: 15 min   **Cook time:** 20 min   **Servings:** 4

Ingredients:

- 4 medium bell peppers, halved and seeded
- 8 oz lean turkey sausage, casings removed
- 4 large eggs
- 1/2 cup spinach, chopped
- 1/4 cup onion, diced
- 1/4 cup low-fat shredded cheddar cheese
- 1 tsp olive oil
- 1 tsp Italian seasoning
- Salt and pepper to taste
- Cooking spray

Directions:

1. Preheat the air fryer to 350°F (175°C).
2. In a pan, cook turkey sausage and onion with olive oil until browned.
3. Add spinach and Italian seasoning and cook until wilted. Set aside.
4. Lightly spray bell pepper halves with cooking spray.
5. Air fry peppers for 5 minutes.
6. Fill each pepper half with sausage mixture.
7. Crack an egg into each pepper half.
8. Air fry for 8-10 minutes until egg whites are set.
9. Sprinkle cheese on top and air fry for 1 more minute.

Serving suggestion: Garnish with fresh herbs and serve with a side salad.

Nutritional information per serving (2 pepper halves): Calories: 270 | Protein: 24g | Carbohydrates: 10g | Fiber: 3g | Net carbs: 7g | Fat: 16g | Cholesterol: 255mg | Sodium: 400mg | Potassium: 450mg

Chickpea Pancakes with Herbs

Prep. time: 10 min | **Cook time:** 16 min | **Servings:** 4 (2 pancakes each)

Ingredients:

- 1 cup chickpea flour
- 1 cup water
- 2 tbsp olive oil
- 1 tsp baking powder
- 1/4 cup mixed fresh herbs (parsley, chives, dill)
- 1 clove garlic, minced
- 1/2 tsp salt
- 1/4 tsp black pepper
- Cooking spray

Directions:

1. Whisk chickpea flour, water, 1 tbsp olive oil, baking powder, herbs, garlic, salt, and pepper in a bowl. Let rest for 5 minutes.
2. Preheat the air fryer to 350°F (175°C).
3. Line the air fryer basket with parchment paper and lightly spray it with cooking spray.
4. Pour 1/4 cup batter for each pancake onto the parchment paper.
5. Air fry for 4 minutes, then carefully flip and cook for another 3-4 minutes until golden.
6. Repeat with the remaining batter.

Serving suggestion: Serve with a dollop of Greek yogurt and mixed greens.

Nutritional information per serving (2 pancakes): Calories: 180 | Protein: 7g | Carbohydrates: 20g | Fiber: 4g | Net carbs: 16g | Fat: 9g | Cholesterol: 0mg | Sodium: 350mg | Potassium: 200mg

Low-Sugar Apple Fritters

Prep. time: 15 min | **Cook time:** 12 min | **Servings:** 4 (2 fritters each)

Ingredients:

- 1 cup almond flour
- 2 tbsp coconut flour
- 2 tsp baking powder
- 1 tsp cinnamon
- 1/4 tsp nutmeg
- 2 tbsp erythritol
- 2 large eggs
- 1/4 cup unsweetened almond milk
- 1 medium apple, finely diced
- 1 tsp vanilla extract
- Cooking spray

Directions:

1. Mix almond flour, coconut flour, baking powder, cinnamon, nutmeg, and erythritol in a bowl.
2. Whisk eggs, almond milk, and vanilla in another bowl.
3. Combine wet and dry ingredients, then fold in a diced apple.
4. Preheat the air fryer to 350°F (175°C).
5. Scoop 1/4 cup batter per fritter onto a parchment-lined air fryer basket.
6. Lightly spray fritters with cooking spray.
7. Air fry for 6 minutes, flip, then cook for another 4-6 minutes until golden.

Serving suggestion: Dust lightly with powdered erythritol if desired.

Nutritional information per serving (2 fritters): Calories: 220 | Protein: 9g | Carbohydrates: 12g | Fiber: 5g | Net carbs: 7g | Fat: 16g | Cholesterol: 95mg | Sodium: 180mg | Potassium: 200mg

Chickpea Avocado Toast

Prep. time: 15 min | Cook time: 15 min | Servings: 4

Ingredients:

- 4 slices whole grain bread
- 1 can (15 oz) chickpeas, drained and rinsed
- 2 ripe avocados
- 1 tbsp lemon juice
- 1 clove garlic, minced
- 1/4 tsp cumin
- Salt and pepper to taste
- 1/4 cup cherry tomatoes, halved
- 2 tbsp red onion, finely diced
- 1 tbsp olive oil
- Cooking spray

Directions:

1. Preheat the air fryer to 400°F (200°C).
2. Toss chickpeas with olive oil, cumin, salt, and pepper.
3. Air fry chickpeas for 10-12 minutes, shaking basket halfway through.
4. Mash avocados with lemon juice, garlic, salt, and pepper.
5. Lightly spray bread slices with cooking spray.
6. Air fry bread at 350°F (175°C) for 3-4 minutes until crispy.
7. Spread avocado mixture on toast and top with crispy chickpeas, tomatoes, and onion.

Serving suggestion: Garnish with fresh herbs like cilantro or parsley.

Nutritional information per serving: Calories: 320 | Protein: 11g | Carbohydrates: 35g | Fiber: 12g | Net carbs: 23g | Fat: 18g | Cholesterol: 0mg | Sodium: 280mg | Potassium: 620mg

Berry Chia Seed Breakfast Bars

Prep. time: 15 min | Cook time: 20 min | Servings: 4

Ingredients:

- 1 cup rolled oats
- 1/4 cup chia seeds
- 1/4 cup almond flour
- 1/4 cup unsweetened shredded coconut
- 1 tsp cinnamon
- 1/4 tsp salt
- 1/4 cup unsweetened applesauce
- 2 tbsp coconut oil, melted
- 2 tbsp erythritol or stevia blend
- 1 large egg
- 1 tsp vanilla extract
- 1/2 cup mixed berries, fresh or frozen

Directions:

1. Mix oats, chia seeds, almond flour, coconut, cinnamon, and salt in a bowl.
2. Whisk applesauce, coconut oil, sweetener, egg, and vanilla in another bowl.
3. Combine wet and dry ingredients. Fold in berries.
4. Line the air fryer basket with parchment paper. Spread the mixture evenly.
5. Air fry at 320°F (160°C) for 20 minutes, until golden and firm.
6. Cool, then cut into 4 bars.

Serving suggestion: Pair with Greek yogurt for added protein.

Nutrition per serving: Calories: 250 | Protein: 7g | Carbohydrates: 20g | Fiber: 8g | Fat: 17g | Cholesterol: 45mg | Sodium: 150mg | Potassium: 180mg

Cauliflower Hash Browns

🥣 **Prep. time:** 15 min 🕐 **Cook time:** 15 min 🍴 **Servings:** 4

Ingredients:

- 1 medium head cauliflower, riced
- 1/4 cup almond flour
- 1 large egg
- 1/4 cup grated Parmesan cheese
- 1 tsp garlic powder
- 1 tsp onion powder
- 1/2 tsp salt
- 1/4 tsp black pepper
- 1 tbsp olive oil

Directions:

1. Rice cauliflower in a food processor or grate by hand.
2. Microwave riced cauliflower for 3 minutes, then drain well.
3. Mix cauliflower with almond flour, egg, cheese, and seasonings.
4. Form the mixture into 8 small patties.
5. Brush the air fryer basket with olive oil.
6. Place patties in the basket, avoiding overlap.
7. Air fry at 380°F (193°C) for 12-15 minutes, flipping halfway.
8. Cook until golden brown and crispy.

Serving suggestion: Serve with a dollop of Greek yogurt and sliced avocado.

Nutrition per serving (2 hash browns): Calories: 120 | Protein: 8g | Carbohydrates: 7g | Fiber: 3g | Fat: 8g | Cholesterol: 55mg | Sodium: 400mg | Potassium: 350mg

Vegetable and Cheese Frittata

🥣 **Prep. time:** 10 min 🕐 **Cook time:** 15 min 🍴 **Servings:** 4

Ingredients:

- 6 large eggs
- 1/4 cup unsweetened almond milk
- 1 cup spinach, chopped
- 1/2 cup bell peppers, diced
- 1/4 cup onion, finely chopped
- 1/2 cup cherry tomatoes, halved
- 1/2 cup low-fat feta cheese, crumbled
- 1 tsp olive oil
- 1/2 tsp dried oregano
- Salt and pepper to taste

Directions:

1. Whisk eggs and almond milk in a bowl. Add salt, pepper, and oregano.
2. Stir in spinach, peppers, onion, tomatoes, and feta.
3. Lightly grease a 7-inch cake pan with olive oil.
4. Pour mixture into the pan.
5. Place pan in air fryer basket.
6. Cook at 300°F (150°C) for 15 minutes or until set and lightly golden.
7. Let cool for 5 minutes before slicing.

Serving suggestion: Pair with a small side salad for extra fiber and nutrients.

Nutrition per serving: Calories: 180 | Protein: 14g | Carbohydrates: 5g | Fiber: 2g | Fat: 12g | Cholesterol: 285mg | Sodium: 300mg | Potassium: 300mg

Almond Flour Banana Bread Slices

Prep. time: 10 min | **Cook time:** 25 min | **Servings:** 4

Ingredients:

- 2 ripe bananas, mashed
- 2 large eggs
- 1/4 cup unsweetened almond milk
- 2 tbsp coconut oil, melted
- 1 1/2 cups almond flour
- 2 tbsp ground flaxseed
- 1 tsp baking powder
- 1 tsp cinnamon
- 1/4 tsp salt
- 2 tbsp erythritol or stevia blend
- 1/4 cup chopped walnuts

Directions:

1. Mix mashed bananas, eggs, almond milk, and coconut oil in a bowl.
2. Combine almond flour, flaxseed, baking powder, cinnamon, salt, and sweetener in another bowl.
3. Combine wet and dry ingredients. Fold in walnuts.
4. Line the air fryer basket with parchment paper.
5. Pour batter into the basket, spreading evenly.
6. Air fry at 310°F (155°C) for 25 minutes or until a toothpick comes out clean.
7. Let cool, then slice into 4 pieces.

Serving suggestion: Enjoy with a small spread of almond butter for added protein.

Nutrition per serving: Calories: 340 | Protein: 12g | Carbohydrates: 18g | Fiber: 6g | Fat: 28g | Cholesterol: 95mg | Sodium: 200mg | Potassium: 280mg

Zucchini and Feta Fritters

Prep. time: 15 min | **Cook time:** 12 min | **Servings:** 4 (3 fritters each)

Ingredients:

- 2 medium zucchinis, grated
- 1/2 cup crumbled feta cheese
- 1/4 cup almond flour
- 1 large egg
- 2 tbsp chopped fresh dill
- 1 clove garlic, minced
- 1/4 tsp salt
- 1/4 tsp black pepper
- 1 tbsp olive oil

Directions:

1. Grate zucchini and squeeze out excess moisture.
2. Mix zucchini with feta, almond flour, egg, dill, garlic, salt, and pepper.
3. Form the mixture into 12 small fritters.
4. Brush the air fryer basket with olive oil.
5. Place fritters in the basket, avoiding overlap.
6. Air fry at 375°F (190°C) for 10-12 minutes, flipping halfway.
7. Cook until golden brown and crispy.

Serving suggestion: Serve with a dollop of Greek yogurt or tzatziki sauce.

Nutrition per serving (3 fritters): Calories: 150 | Protein: 8g | Carbohydrates: 6g | Fiber: 2g | Fat: 11g | Cholesterol: 65mg | Sodium: 350mg | Potassium: 300mg

Breakfast Pizza on Cauliflower Crust

Prep. time: 20 min | **Cook time:** 20 min | **Servings:** 4

Ingredients:

For the crust:
- 2 cups riced cauliflower
- 1 large egg
- 1/4 cup grated Parmesan cheese
- 1/4 tsp garlic powder
- 1/4 tsp salt

For the toppings:
- 1/4 cup sugar-free tomato sauce
- 1/2 cup shredded mozzarella cheese
- 4 large eggs
- 1/4 cup diced bell peppers
- 1/4 cup sliced mushrooms
- 2 tbsp chopped fresh basil
- 1 tsp olive oil

Directions:

1. Rice cauliflower in a food processor. Microwave for 5 minutes, then drain well.
2. Mix cauliflower with egg, Parmesan, garlic powder, and salt.
3. Press the mixture into a parchment-lined air fryer basket, forming a crust.
4. Air fry at 380°F (193°C) for 10 minutes until golden.
5. Spread tomato sauce on the crust and top with cheese and vegetables.
6. Create 4 wells in the toppings and add an egg.
7. Air fry at 350°F (175°C) for 8-10 minutes until eggs are set.
8. Sprinkle with basil and drizzle with olive oil before serving.

Serving suggestion: Pair with a small side of mixed greens for added nutrients.

Nutrition per serving: Calories: 220 | Protein: 18g | Carbohydrates: 8g | Fiber: 3g | Fat: 14g | Cholesterol: 240mg | Sodium: 450mg | Potassium: 350mg

Peanut Butter and Jelly Protein Bars

Prep. time: 15 min | **Cook time:** 12 min | **Servings:** 4

Ingredients:

- 1 cup almond flour
- 1/4 cup unflavoured whey protein powder
- 1/4 cup natural peanut butter
- 2 tbsp ground flaxseed
- 2 tbsp erythritol or stevia blend
- 1 large egg
- 1 tsp vanilla extract
- 1/4 cup sugar-free strawberry jam
- 1 tbsp chia seeds

Directions:

1. Mix almond flour, protein powder, flaxseed, and sweetener in a bowl.
2. Add peanut butter, egg, and vanilla. Mix to form a dough.
3. Press 2/3 of the dough into a parchment-lined air fryer basket.
4. Mix jam with chia seeds and spread over the dough.
5. Crumble the remaining dough on top.
6. Air fry at 320°F (160°C) for 12 minutes, until golden.
7. Cool completely before cutting into 4 bars.

Serving suggestion: Pair with a small serving of Greek yogurt for added protein.

Nutrition per serving: Calories: 280 | Protein: 15g | Carbohydrates: 12g | Fiber: 6g | Fat: 21g | Cholesterol: 50mg | Sodium: 95mg | Potassium: 200mg

Coconut Flour Blueberry Muffins

Prep. time: 10 min | **Cook time:** 15 min | **Servings:** 4 (2 muffins each)

Ingredients:

- 1/2 cup coconut flour
- 1/4 cup erythritol or stevia blend
- 1 tsp baking powder
- 1/4 tsp salt
- 4 large eggs
- 1/4 cup coconut oil, melted
- 1/4 cup unsweetened almond milk
- 1 tsp vanilla extract
- 1/2 cup fresh blueberries
- 1/4 cup chopped walnuts

Directions:

1. Mix coconut flour, sweetener, baking powder, and salt in a bowl.
2. Whisk eggs, coconut oil, almond milk, and vanilla in another bowl.
3. Combine wet and dry ingredients. Fold in blueberries and walnuts.
4. Line the air fryer basket with 8 silicone muffin cups.
5. Divide batter among cups.
6. Air fry at 300°F (150°C) for 15 minutes until a toothpick comes out clean.
7. Let cool before removing from cups.

Serving suggestion: Enjoy with a small spread of almond butter for added protein.

Nutrition per serving (2 muffins): Calories: 260 | Protein: 9g | Carbohydrates: 11g | Fiber: 6g | Fat: 21g | Cholesterol: 185mg | Sodium: 230mg | Potassium: 150mg

Egg and Cheese Stuffed Tomatoes

Prep. time: 10 min | **Cook time:** 15 min | **Servings:** 4

Ingredients:

- 4 medium tomatoes
- 4 large eggs
- 1/4 cup shredded low-fat cheddar cheese
- 2 tbsp chopped fresh basil
- 2 tbsp grated Parmesan cheese
- 1/4 tsp garlic powder
- Salt and pepper to taste
- 1 tsp olive oil

Directions:

1. Cut tops off tomatoes and scoop out seeds and pulp.
2. Mix cheddar, basil, Parmesan, garlic powder, salt, and pepper in a bowl.
3. Sprinkle cheese mixture inside tomatoes.
4. Crack an egg into each tomato.
5. Brush the air fryer basket with olive oil.
6. Place stuffed tomatoes in the basket.
7. Air fry at 350°F (175°C) for 12-15 minutes until egg whites are set.

Serving suggestion: Pair with a small side salad for added fiber and nutrients.

Nutrition per serving (1 stuffed tomato): Calories: 140 | Protein: 11g | Carbohydrates: 5g | Fiber: 1g | Fat: 9g | Cholesterol: 195mg | Sodium: 180mg | Potassium: 350mg

Zucchini and Carrot Morning Glory Muffins

Prep. time: 15 min | **Cook time:** 15 min | **Servings:** 4 (2 muffins each)

Ingredients:

- 1 cup almond flour
- 1/4 cup coconut flour
- 2 tbsp ground flaxseed
- 1 tsp baking powder
- 1 tsp cinnamon
- 1/4 tsp salt
- 3 large eggs
- 1/4 cup unsweetened applesauce
- 2 tbsp coconut oil, melted
- 2 tbsp erythritol or stevia blend
- 1/2 cup grated zucchini
- 1/4 cup grated carrot
- 2 tbsp chopped walnuts
- 2 tbsp unsweetened shredded coconut

Directions:

1. Mix dry ingredients in a bowl: almond flour, coconut flour, flaxseed, baking powder, cinnamon, and salt.
2. Whisk eggs, applesauce, coconut oil, and sweetener in another bowl.
3. Combine wet and dry ingredients. Fold in zucchini, carrot, walnuts, and coconut.
4. Line the air fryer basket with 8 silicone muffin cups.
5. Divide batter among cups.
6. Air fry at 310°F (155°C) for 15 minutes until a toothpick emerges.
7. Let cool before removing from cups.

Serving suggestion: Enjoy with a small spread of almond butter for added protein.

Nutrition per serving (2 muffins): Calories: 290 | Protein: 10g | Carbohydrates: 14g | Fiber: 7g | Fat: 23g | Cholesterol: 140mg | Sodium: 220mg | Potassium: 200mg

Breakfast Burrito Bowl

Prep. time: 15 min | **Cook time:** 20 min | **Servings:** 4

Ingredients:

- 1 medium cauliflower, riced
- 1 tbsp olive oil
- 1 tsp cumin
- 1/2 tsp chili powder
- Salt and pepper to taste
- 1 bell pepper, diced
- 1 small onion, diced
- 8 large eggs
- 1 cup black beans, drained and rinsed
- 1 avocado, sliced
- 1/4 cup low-fat shredded cheddar cheese
- 1/4 cup fresh cilantro, chopped
- 1 lime, cut into wedges

Directions:

1. Toss riced cauliflower with 1/2 tbsp oil, cumin, chili powder, salt, and pepper.
2. Air fry cauliflower at 380°F (193°C) for 10 minutes, shaking basket halfway.
3. Mix peppers and onions with remaining oil. Add to air fryer with cauliflower.
4. Cook for another 5 minutes until vegetables are tender.
5. Whisk eggs and season with salt and pepper.
6. Pour eggs into a greased air fryer-safe pan.
7. Air fry at 300°F (150°C) for 5-7 minutes until set, stirring once halfway.
8. Divide cauliflower rice among 4 bowls. Top with scrambled eggs, black beans, air-fried vegetables, avocado, cheese, and cilantro.
9. Serve with lime wedges.

Serving suggestion: Add a spoonful of Greek yogurt for extra protein and creaminess.
Nutrition per serving: Calories: 380 | Protein: 24g | Carbohydrates: 25g | Fiber: 12g | Fat: 23g | Cholesterol: 380mg | Sodium: 400mg | Potassium: 800mg

Blueberry Lemon Scones

Prep. time: 15 min   **Cook time:** 12 min   **Servings:** 4 (1 scone each)

Ingredients:

- 1 cup almond flour
- 1/4 cup coconut flour
- 2 tbsp ground flaxseed
- 1 tsp baking powder
- 1/4 tsp salt
- 2 tbsp erythritol or stevia blend
- Zest of 1 lemon
- 1/4 cup cold unsalted butter, cubed
- 1 large egg
- 2 tbsp unsweetened almond milk
- 1/2 tsp vanilla extract
- 1/3 cup fresh blueberries

Directions:

1. Mix dry ingredients, sweetener, and lemon zest in a bowl.
2. Cut in cold butter until the mixture resembles coarse crumbs.
3. Whisk egg, almond milk, and vanilla in another bowl.
4. Combine wet and dry ingredients. Gently fold in blueberries.
5. Form dough into a round disk, cut into 4 wedges.
6. Line the air fryer basket with parchment paper.
7. Place scones in the basket, leaving space between each.
8. Air fry at 320°F (160°C) for 12 minutes, until golden brown.

Serving suggestion: Enjoy with a small spread of sugar-free lemon curd or Greek yogurt.

Nutrition per serving (1 scone): Calories: 290 | Protein: 9g | Carbohydrates: 12g | Fiber: 6g | Fat: 24g | Cholesterol: 70mg | Sodium: 220mg | Potassium: 180mg

Breakfast Sweet Potato Boats

Prep. time: 10 min   **Cook time:** 25 min   **Servings:** 4

Ingredients:

- 2 medium sweet potatoes
- 4 large eggs
- 1/4 cup crumbled feta cheese
- 1/4 cup diced bell peppers
- 2 tbsp chopped fresh spinach
- 2 tbsp chopped green onions
- 1 tsp olive oil
- 1/4 tsp smoked paprika
- Salt and pepper to taste

Directions:

1. Wash sweet potatoes and prick them with a fork several times.
2. Air fry at 400°F (200°C) for 20 minutes, turning halfway.
3. Let cool slightly, then cut in half lengthwise.
4. Scoop out some flesh, leaving a 1/4-inch border.
5. Brush the insides with olive oil and sprinkle with paprika, salt, and pepper.
6. Divide bell peppers, spinach, and green onions among boats.
7. Crack an egg into each boat.
8. Air fry at 350°F (175°C) for 5-7 minutes until egg whites are set.
9. Sprinkle with feta cheese before serving.

Serving suggestion: Pair with a side of mixed berries for added antioxidants.

Nutrition per serving (1 sweet potato boat): Calories: 180 | Protein: 10g | Carbohydrates: 18g | Fiber: 3g | Fat: 9g | Cholesterol: 195mg | Sodium: 220mg | Potassium: 450mg

Greek-Style Spinach and Olive Breakfast Muffins

Prep. time: 15 min | **Cook time:** 12 min | **Servings:** 4 (2 muffins each)

Ingredients:

- 1 cup almond flour
- 1/4 cup coconut flour
- 1 tsp baking powder
- 1/4 tsp salt
- 4 large eggs
- 1/4 cup olive oil
- 1/4 cup unsweetened almond milk
- 1 cup fresh spinach, chopped
- 1/4 cup Kalamata olives, chopped
- 1/4 cup crumbled feta cheese
- 1 tsp dried oregano
- 1/2 tsp garlic powder

Directions:

1. Mix almond flour, coconut flour, baking powder, and salt in a bowl.
2. Whisk eggs, olive oil, and almond milk in another bowl.
3. Combine wet and dry ingredients. Fold in spinach, olives, feta, oregano, and garlic powder.
4. Line the air fryer basket with 8 silicone muffin cups.
5. Divide batter among cups.
6. Air fry at 320°F (160°C) for 12 minutes until a toothpick comes out clean.
7. Let cool before removing from cups.

Serving suggestion: Pair with a small Greek yogurt for added protein.

Nutrition per serving (2 muffins): Calories: 340 | Protein: 13g | Carbohydrates: 10g | Fiber: 5g | Fat: 29g | Cholesterol: 190mg | Sodium: 450mg | Potassium: 200mg

Pecan Pie Granola Bars

Prep. time: 10 min | **Cook time:** 15 min | **Servings:** 4 (1 bar each)

Ingredients:

- 1 cup rolled oats
- 1/2 cup chopped pecans
- 1/4 cup ground flaxseed
- 2 tbsp erythritol or stevia blend
- 1 tsp cinnamon
- 1/4 tsp salt
- 1/4 cup unsweetened applesauce
- 2 tbsp almond butter
- 1 tsp vanilla extract
- 1 large egg white

Directions:

1. Mix oats, pecans, flaxseed, sweetener, cinnamon, and salt in a bowl.
2. Whisk applesauce, almond butter, vanilla, and egg white in another bowl.
3. Combine wet and dry ingredients.
4. Line the air fryer basket with parchment paper.
5. Press the mixture into the basket, forming a compact rectangle.
6. Air fry at 300°F (150°C) for 15 minutes, until golden and firm.
7. Let cool completely before cutting into 4 bars.

Serving suggestion: Enjoy with a small serving of Greek yogurt for added protein.

Nutrition per serving (1 bar): Calories: 250 | Protein: 8g | Carbohydrates: 20g | Fiber: 6g | Fat: 17g | Cholesterol: 0mg | Sodium: 150mg | Potassium: 200mg

Salads

Crunchy Greens Salad with Grilled Chicken and Herbs

Prep. time: 15 min | **Cook time:** 15 min | **Servings:** 4

Ingredients:

- 1 lb boneless, skinless chicken breast
- 8 cups mixed salad greens
- 1 cup cherry tomatoes, halved
- 1 cucumber, sliced
- 1/4 cup red onion, thinly sliced
- 1/4 cup pumpkin seeds
- 2 tbsp olive oil
- 1 tbsp lemon juice
- 1 tsp dried herbs (oregano, thyme, rosemary mix)
- Salt and pepper to taste
- Cooking spray

Directions:

1. Preheat the air fryer to 380°F (190°C).
2. Season chicken with 1 tbsp olive oil, herbs, salt, and pepper.
3. Air fry chicken for 12-15 minutes, flipping halfway until internal temperature reaches 165°F (74°C).
4. While chicken cooks, prepare salad greens, tomatoes, cucumber, and onion in a large bowl.
5. In a small bowl, whisk the remaining olive oil, lemon juice, salt, and pepper for dressing.
6. Slice cooked chicken.
7. Toss salad with dressing and top with chicken and pumpkin seeds.

Serving suggestion: Garnish with additional fresh herbs if desired.

Nutritional information per serving: Calories: 280 | Protein: 29g | Carbohydrates: 10g | Fiber: 4g | Net carbs: 6g | Fat: 15g | Cholesterol: 70mg | Sodium: 220mg | Potassium: 700mg

Mediterranean Tuna Salad with Fresh Herbs

Prep. time: 15 min | **Cook time:** 10 min | **Servings:** 4

Ingredients:

- 2 cans (5 oz each) chunk light tuna in water, drained
- 1 cup cherry tomatoes, halved
- 1 cucumber, diced
- 1/4 cup red onion, finely chopped
- 1/4 cup kalamata olives, pitted and chopped
- 1/4 cup fresh parsley, chopped
- 2 tbsp fresh mint, chopped
- 2 tbsp olive oil
- 1 tbsp lemon juice
- 1 tsp dried oregano
- Salt and pepper to taste
- 1 cup chickpeas, drained and rinsed
- Cooking spray

Directions:

1. Preheat the air fryer to 390°F (200°C).
2. Pat chickpeas dry, spray with cooking spray, season with salt and oregano.
3. Air fry chickpeas for 8-10 minutes, shaking basket halfway through, until crispy.
4. Mix a large bowl of tuna, tomatoes, cucumber, onion, olives, parsley, and mint.
5. Whisk olive oil, lemon juice, salt, and pepper in a small bowl for dressing.
6. Toss salad with dressing and top with crispy chickpeas.

Serving suggestion: Serve over a bed of mixed greens or with cucumber slices for scooping.

Nutritional information per serving: Calories: 250 | Protein: 20g | Carbohydrates: 15g | Fiber: 5g | Net carbs: 10g | Fat: 13g | Cholesterol: 30mg | Sodium: 400mg | Potassium: 450mg

Spinach & Strawberry Salad with Balsamic Vinaigrette

Prep. time: 15 min   **Cook time:** 10 min   **Servings:** 4

Ingredients:

- 6 cups fresh baby spinach
- 1 cup fresh strawberries, sliced
- 1/4 cup red onion, thinly sliced
- 1/4 cup pecans, raw
- 2 oz goat cheese, crumbled

For the dressing:

- 2 tbsp extra virgin olive oil
- 1 tbsp balsamic vinegar
- 1 tsp Dijon mustard
- 1 tsp erythritol or stevia (to taste)
- Salt and pepper to taste

Directions:

1. Preheat the air fryer to 300°F (150°C).
2. Place pecans in the air fryer basket in a single layer. Cook for 3-4 minutes, shaking halfway through, until lightly toasted. Set aside to cool.
3. To make the dressing, whisk together olive oil, balsamic vinegar, Dijon mustard, erythritol or stevia, salt, and pepper in a small bowl.
4. Combine spinach, sliced strawberries, and red onion in a large bowl.
5. Drizzle the dressing over the salad and toss gently to coat.
6. Divide the salad among four plates. Top each serving with toasted pecans and crumbled goat cheese.

Serving suggestion: Serve immediately as a light meal or as a side dish with grilled chicken or fish for added protein.

Nutritional Information (per serving): Calories: 180 | Protein: 5g | Carbohydrates: 10g | Fiber: 3g | Sugar: 4g | Fat: 14g (mostly healthy fats from olive oil and nuts) | Cholesterol: 7mg | Sodium: 120mg | Potassium: 350mg

Low-Carb Caesar Salad with Shrimp

Prep. time: 20 min   **Cook time:** 10 min   **Servings:** 4

Ingredients:

- 8 cups romaine lettuce, chopped
- 1 lb medium shrimp, peeled and deveined
- 1 tbsp olive oil
- 1 tsp garlic powder
- 1/4 cup grated Parmesan cheese
- 1/4 cup almond flour
- Salt and pepper to taste

Low-Carb Caesar Dressing:

- 1/3 cup mayonnaise
- 1 tbsp lemon juice
- 1 tsp Dijon mustard
- 1 tsp Worcestershire sauce
- 1 clove garlic, minced
- 2 tbsp grated Parmesan cheese
- Salt and pepper to taste

Directions:

1. Preheat the air fryer to 400°F (200°C).
2. Toss shrimp with olive oil, garlic powder, salt, and pepper in a bowl.
3. Place shrimp in a single layer in an air fryer basket. Cook for 5-6 minutes, shaking halfway through, until pink and cooked through. Set aside.
4. Mix almond flour and 1/4 cup Parmesan cheese in a small bowl.
5. Spray the air fryer basket with oil. Add almond flour mixture and cook at 350°F (175°C) for 2-3 minutes, shaking every minute, until golden. This creates a low-carb "crouton" topping.
6. For the dressing, whisk all dressing ingredients in a bowl.
7. In a large bowl, toss romaine lettuce with dressing.
8. Divide lettuce among four plates. Top with air-fried shrimp and sprinkle with almond flour "croutons."

Serving suggestion: Serve immediately. For added nutrition, consider adding sliced cherry tomatoes or cucumber.

Nutritional Information (per serving): Calories: 350 | Protein: 28g | Carbohydrates: 6g | Fiber: 3g | Sugar: 1g | Fat: 25g (mostly healthy fats) | Cholesterol: 180mg | Sodium: 550mg | Potassium: 400mg

Grilled Salmon Kale Salad with Lemon Dressing

Prep. time: 15 min **Cook time:** 12 min **Servings:** 4

Ingredients:

- 4 (4 oz) salmon fillets
- 8 cups kale, chopped
- 1 medium avocado, sliced
- 1/4 cup pumpkin seeds
- 1 tbsp olive oil
- 1 tsp garlic powder
- Salt and pepper to taste
- 3 tbsp extra virgin olive oil
- 2 tbsp fresh lemon juice
- 1 tsp Dijon mustard
- 1 clove garlic, minced
- 1/4 tsp stevia (or to taste)
- Salt and pepper to taste

Directions:

1. Preheat the air fryer to 400°F (200°C).
2. Rub salmon fillets with olive oil, garlic powder, salt, and pepper.
3. Place salmon in an air fryer basket, skin-side down. Cook for 8-10 minutes until flaky.
4. While salmon cooks, massage kale with olive oil to soften.
5. In a small bowl, whisk together all dressing ingredients.
6. Once the salmon is done, remove it and let it cool slightly.
7. Toss kale with dressing in a large bowl.
8. Divide kale among four plates. Top with salmon, avocado slices, and pumpkin seeds.

Serving suggestion: Serve immediately. For added flavor, squeeze fresh lemon over the salmon.

Nutritional Information (per serving): Calories: 420 | Protein: 28g | Carbohydrates: 12g | Fiber: 6g | Sugar: 1g | Fat: 32g (mostly healthy fats) | Cholesterol: 60mg | Sodium: 200mg | Potassium: 900mg

Asian Style Broccoli Slaw with Crunchy Tofu

Prep. time: 20 min **Cook time:** 15 min **Servings:** 4

Ingredients:

- 1 block (14 oz) extra-firm tofu, pressed and cubed
- 4 cups broccoli slaw mix
- 1 red bell pepper, thinly sliced
- 1/4 cup unsalted peanuts, chopped
- 2 tbsp cornstarch (for coating tofu)
- 1 tbsp sesame oil
- Salt and pepper to taste
- 2 tbsp rice vinegar
- 1 tbsp low-sodium soy sauce
- 1 tbsp sesame oil
- 1 tsp grated ginger
- 1 clove garlic, minced
- 1 tsp erythritol or stevia (to taste)
- 1/4 tsp red pepper flakes (optional)

Directions:

1. Preheat the air fryer to 375°F (190°C).
2. Toss tofu cubes with cornstarch, salt, and pepper.
3. Lightly brush the air fryer basket with sesame oil. Add tofu in a single layer.
4. Cook tofu for 12-15 minutes, shaking basket every 5 minutes, until golden and crispy.
5. Whisk all dressing ingredients in a small bowl while tofu cooks.
6. Add broccoli slaw mix and bell pepper in a large bowl.
7. Toss slaw with dressing.
8. Divide slaw among four plates. Top with crispy tofu and chopped peanuts.

Serving suggestion: Garnish with fresh cilantro or green onions if desired.

Nutritional Information (per serving): Calories: 250 | Protein: 15g | Carbohydrates: 15g | Fiber: 5g | Sugar: 4g | Fat: 16g (mostly healthy fats) | Cholesterol: 0mg | Sodium: 280mg | Potassium: 450mg

Fresh Garden Vegetable Quinoa Bowl

Prep. time: 15 min **Cook time:** 20 min **Servings:** 4

Ingredients:

- 1 cup uncooked quinoa
- 2 cups mixed vegetables (zucchini, bell peppers, cherry tomatoes)
- 1 can (15 oz) chickpeas, drained and rinsed
- 1 tbsp olive oil
- 1 tsp garlic powder
- 1 tsp dried oregano
- Salt and pepper to taste

Lemon-Herb Dressing:
- 2 tbsp extra virgin olive oil
- 2 tbsp lemon juice
- 1 tsp Dijon mustard
- 1 clove garlic, minced
- 1 tbsp fresh herbs (parsley, basil, or cilantro), chopped
- Salt and pepper to taste

Directions:

1. Cook quinoa according to package instructions. Set aside.
2. Preheat the air fryer to 400°F (200°C).
3. In a bowl, toss vegetables and chickpeas with olive oil, garlic powder, oregano, salt, and pepper.
4. Place the mixture in the air fryer basket. Cook for 12-15 minutes, shaking basket every 5 minutes, until vegetables are tender and lightly charred.
5. Whisk together all dressing ingredients in a small bowl while the vegetables cook.
6. Divide cooked quinoa into four bowls. Top with air-fried vegetables and chickpeas.
7. Drizzle with lemon-herb dressing before serving.

Serving suggestion: Garnish with additional fresh herbs or a desired sprinkle of feta cheese.
Nutritional Information (per serving): Calories: 320 | Protein: 12g | Carbohydrates: 45g | Fiber: 8g | Sugar: 4g | Fat: 13g (mostly healthy fats) | Cholesterol: 0mg | Sodium: 200mg | Potassium: 500mg

Marinated Artichoke Heart and Shrimp Pasta-Salad

Prep. time: 20 min **Cook time:** 15 min **Servings:** 4

Ingredients:

- 8 oz whole wheat penne pasta
- 1 lb medium shrimp, peeled and deveined
- 1 can (14 oz) artichoke hearts, drained and quartered
- 1 cup cherry tomatoes, halved
- 2 cups baby spinach
- 1 tbsp olive oil
- 1 tsp garlic powder
- 1 tsp dried oregano
- Salt and pepper to taste

Lemon-Herb Dressing:
- 3 tbsp extra virgin olive oil
- 2 tbsp lemon juice
- 1 tsp Dijon mustard
- 1 clove garlic, minced
- 1 tbsp fresh parsley, chopped
- Salt and pepper to taste

Directions:

1. Cook pasta according to package instructions. Drain and set aside to cool.
2. Preheat the air fryer to 400°F (200°C).
3. In a bowl, toss shrimp with olive oil, garlic powder, oregano, salt, and pepper.
4. Place shrimp in a single layer in an air fryer basket. Cook for 5-6 minutes, shaking halfway through, until pink and cooked through. Set aside to cool.
5. Add artichoke hearts and cherry tomatoes in the same air fryer basket. Cook for 5 minutes at 380°F (193°C), shaking halfway through, until lightly charred.
6. In a large bowl, whisk together all dressing ingredients.
7. Add cooled pasta, air-fried shrimp, artichokes, tomatoes, and fresh spinach to the bowl with dressing. Toss gently to combine.
8. Chill for at least 30 minutes before serving.

Serving suggestion: Garnish with additional fresh parsley and a lemon wedge if desired.
Nutritional Information (per serving): Calories: 380 | Protein: 25g | Carbohydrates: 40g | Fiber: 7g | Sugar: 3g | Fat: 16g (mostly healthy fats) | Cholesterol: 145mg | Sodium: 350mg | Potassium: 500mg

Summer Berry Almond Spinach Salad

🥣 **Prep. time:** 15 min   🕐 **Cook time:** 5 min   🍴 **Servings:** 4

Ingredients:

- 8 cups fresh baby spinach
- 1 cup mixed berries (strawberries, blueberries, raspberries)
- 1/4 cup red onion, thinly sliced
- 1/2 cup sliced almonds
- 2 oz goat cheese, crumbled

Berry Vinaigrette:

- 1/4 cup fresh mixed berries
- 2 tbsp extra virgin olive oil
- 1 tbsp apple cider vinegar
- 1 tsp Dijon mustard
- 1 tsp erythritol or stevia (to taste)
- Salt and pepper to taste

Directions:

1. Preheat the air fryer to 300°F (150°C).
2. Spread sliced almonds in the air fryer basket in a single layer. Cook for 3-4 minutes, shaking halfway through, until lightly toasted. Set aside to cool.
3. Combine all vinaigrette ingredients in a blender until smooth.
4. Combine spinach, mixed berries, and red onion in a large bowl.
5. Drizzle the vinaigrette over the salad and toss gently to coat.
6. Divide the salad among four plates. Top each serving with toasted almonds and crumbled goat cheese.

Serving suggestion: Serve immediately as a light meal or as a side dish with grilled chicken or fish for added protein.

Nutritional Information (per serving): Calories: 200 | Protein: 7g | Carbohydrates: 12g | Fiber: 5g | Sugar: 5g | Fat: 15g (mostly healthy fats from olive oil and almonds) | Cholesterol: 5mg | Sodium: 110mg | Potassium: 450mg

Roasted Pumpkin and Arugula Superfood Bowl

🥣 **Prep. time:** 15 min   🕐 **Cook time:** 20 min   🍴 **Servings:** 4

Ingredients:

- 2 cups pumpkin, cubed
- 4 cups arugula
- 1/2 cup quinoa, uncooked
- 1/4 cup pumpkin seeds
- 1/4 cup dried cranberries, unsweetened
- 1 tbsp olive oil
- 1 tsp cinnamon
- Salt and pepper to taste

Maple-Dijon Dressing:

- 2 tbsp extra virgin olive oil
- 1 tbsp apple cider vinegar
- 1 tsp Dijon mustard
- 1 tsp sugar-free maple syrup
- Salt and pepper to taste

Directions:

1. Preheat the air fryer to 400°F (200°C).
2. Toss pumpkin cubes with olive oil, cinnamon, salt, and pepper.
3. Place pumpkin in air fryer basket. Cook for 15-20 minutes, shaking every 5 minutes, until tender and lightly browned.
4. Meanwhile, cook quinoa according to package instructions. Set aside to cool.
5. In a small bowl, whisk together all dressing ingredients.
6. Combine arugula, cooled quinoa, and roasted pumpkin in a large bowl.
7. Add pumpkin seeds and dried cranberries.
8. Drizzle with dressing and toss gently to combine.

Serving suggestion: Divide among four bowls. For added protein, top with grilled chicken or tofu.

Nutritional Information (per serving): Calories: 280 | Protein: 8g | Carbohydrates: 35g | Fiber: 6g | Sugar: 5g | Fat: 15g (mostly healthy fats) | Cholesterol: 0mg | Sodium: 150mg | Potassium: 450mg

Grilled Chicken and Avocado Salad

Prep. time: 15 min | **Cook time:** 12 min | **Servings:** 4

Ingredients:

- 1 lb chicken breast, cut into strips
- 4 cups mixed salad greens
- 2 medium avocados, sliced
- 1 cup cherry tomatoes, halved
- 1/4 cup red onion, thinly sliced
- 2 tbsp olive oil
- 1 tbsp lemon juice
- 1 tsp dried oregano
- 1/2 tsp garlic powder
- Salt and pepper to taste

Dressing:
- 2 tbsp extra virgin olive oil
- 1 tbsp apple cider vinegar
- 1 tsp Dijon mustard
- 1 tsp erythritol

Directions:

1. Mix olive oil, lemon juice, oregano, garlic powder, salt, and pepper. Coat chicken strips.
2. Preheat air fryer to 380°F (193°C).
3. Place chicken strips in an air fryer basket without overcrowding.
4. Cook for 10-12 minutes, shaking basket halfway through.
5. Prepare salad with greens, avocado, tomatoes, and onion.
6. Whisk dressing ingredients in a small bowl.
7. Top salad with cooked chicken and drizzle with dressing.

Serving suggestion: Pair with a small portion of quinoa for added fiber and nutrients.

Nutrition per serving: Calories: 380 | Protein: 29g | Carbohydrates: 12g | Fiber: 8g | Fat: 26g | Cholesterol: 73mg | Sodium: 220mg | Potassium: 850mg

Warm Salmon Niçoise Salad

Prep. time: 15 min | **Cook time:** 15 min | **Servings:** 4

Ingredients:

- 4 (4 oz) salmon fillets
- 8 cups mixed salad greens
- 8 oz green beans, trimmed
- 1 cup cherry tomatoes, halved
- 1/2 cup Kalamata olives, pitted
- 2 hard-boiled eggs, quartered
- 1 tbsp olive oil
- 1 tsp dried herbs de Provence
- Salt and pepper to taste

Dressing:
- 2 tbsp extra virgin olive oil
- 1 tbsp Dijon mustard
- 1 tbsp lemon juice
- 1 tsp capers, minced
- 1 small garlic clove, minced

Directions:

1. Brush salmon with olive oil, season with herbs, salt, and pepper.
2. Preheat the air fryer to 400°F (200°C).
3. Air fry salmon for 8-10 minutes until flaky.
4. Air fry green beans at 380°F (193°C) for 5-7 minutes, shaking basket halfway.
5. Arrange salad greens, tomatoes, olives, and eggs on plates.
6. Top with warm salmon and green beans.
7. Whisk dressing ingredients and drizzle over salad.

Serving suggestion: Add a small portion of quinoa for extra fiber if desired.

Nutrition per serving: Calories: 420 | Protein: 32g | Carbohydrates: 10g | Fiber: 5g | Fat: 28g | Cholesterol: 160mg | Sodium: 450mg | Potassium: 920mg

Spicy Sweet Potato and Black Bean Salad

Prep. time: 15 min   **Cook time:** 20 min   **Servings:** 4

Ingredients:

- 2 medium sweet potatoes, cubed
- 1 can (15 oz) black beans, drained and rinsed
- 1 red bell pepper, diced
- 1/4 cup red onion, finely chopped
- 2 tbsp olive oil
- 1 tsp smoked paprika
- 1/2 tsp ground cumin
- 1/4 tsp cayenne pepper
- Salt to taste
- 2 cups mixed salad greens
- 1/4 cup cilantro, chopped

- 2 tbsp lime juice
- 1 tbsp olive oil
- 1 tsp honey
- 1/4 tsp ground cumin

Directions:

1. Toss sweet potatoes with 1 tbsp olive oil, paprika, cumin, cayenne, and salt.
2. Preheat the air fryer to 400°F (200°C).
3. Air fry sweet potatoes for 15-20 minutes, shaking basket every 5 minutes.
4. Mix black beans, bell pepper, and onion in a bowl.
5. Add air-fried sweet potatoes to the bean mixture.
6. Whisk dressing ingredients and drizzle over the salad.
7. Serve over mixed greens and garnish with cilantro.

Serving suggestion: Add a dollop of Greek yogurt for extra protein.

Nutrition per serving: Calories: 280 | Protein: 10g | Carbohydrates: 40g | Fiber: 12g | Fat: 11g | Cholesterol: 0mg | Sodium: 300mg | Potassium: 700mg

Asparagus and Goat Cheese Salad

Prep. time: 10 min   **Cook time:** 8 min   **Servings:** 4

Ingredients:

- 1 lb asparagus, trimmed
- 4 cups mixed salad greens
- 2 oz soft goat cheese, crumbled
- 1/4 cup walnuts, chopped
- 1 tbsp olive oil
- 1 tsp lemon zest
- Salt and pepper to taste

Dressing:

- 2 tbsp extra virgin olive oil
- 1 tbsp lemon juice
- 1 tsp Dijon mustard
- 1 small garlic clove, minced

Directions:

1. Toss asparagus with 1 tbsp olive oil, lemon zest, salt, and pepper.
2. Preheat the air fryer to 400°F (200°C).
3. Air fry asparagus for 6-8 minutes, shaking basket halfway through.
4. Arrange salad greens on plates.
5. Top with air-fried asparagus, crumbled goat cheese, and walnuts.
6. Whisk dressing ingredients and drizzle over salad.

Serving suggestion: Pair with a small portion of grilled chicken for extra protein.

Nutrition per serving: Calories: 200 | Protein: 7g | Carbohydrates: 8g | Fiber: 4g | Fat: 17g | Cholesterol: 7mg | Sodium: 120mg | Potassium: 350mg

Warm Mediterranean Vegetable Salad

Prep. time: 15 min　**Cook time:** 15 min　**Servings:** 4

Ingredients:

- 1 medium eggplant, cubed
- 1 red bell pepper, sliced
- 1 zucchini, sliced
- 1 red onion, sliced
- 2 tbsp olive oil
- 1 tsp dried oregano
- 1 tsp dried basil
- 4 cups mixed salad greens
- 1/4 cup Kalamata olives, pitted
- 2 oz feta cheese, crumbled

Dressing:

- 2 tbsp extra virgin olive oil
- 1 tbsp balsamic vinegar
- 1 tsp Dijon mustard
- 1 clove garlic, minced

Directions:

Instructions:

1. Toss vegetables with 2 tbsp olive oil, oregano, basil, salt, and pepper.
2. Preheat the air fryer to 380°F (193°C).
3. Air fry vegetables for 12-15 minutes, shaking basket every 5 minutes.
4. Arrange salad greens on plates.
5. Top with warm air-fried vegetables, olives, and feta.
6. Whisk dressing ingredients and drizzle over salad.

Serving suggestion: Add grilled chicken or chickpeas for extra protein.

Nutrition per serving: Calories: 240 | Protein: 5g | Carbohydrates: 15g | Fiber: 7g | Fat: 19g | Cholesterol: 11mg | Sodium: 350mg | Potassium: 600mg

Crispy Air-Fried Chickpea Salad

Prep. time: 10 min　**Cook time:** 15 min　**Servings:** 4

Ingredients:

- 1 can (15 oz) chickpeas, drained and rinsed
- 1 tbsp olive oil
- 1 tsp smoked paprika
- 1/2 tsp cumin
- 1/4 tsp garlic powder
- Salt and pepper to taste
- 6 cups mixed salad greens
- 1 cucumber, sliced
- 1 cup cherry tomatoes, halved
- 1/4 red onion, thinly sliced

Dressing:

- 2 tbsp lemon juice
- 1 tbsp olive oil
- 1 tsp Dijon mustard
- 1 small garlic clove, minced

Directions:

1. Pat chickpeas dry with paper towels.
2. Toss chickpeas with 1 tbsp olive oil, paprika, cumin, garlic powder, salt, and pepper.
3. Preheat the air fryer to 390°F (200°C).
4. Air fry chickpeas for 12-15 minutes, shaking basket every 5 minutes until crispy.
5. Arrange salad greens, cucumber, tomatoes, and onion on plates.
6. Top with crispy chickpeas.
7. Whisk dressing ingredients and drizzle over salad.

Serving suggestion: Add a dollop of Greek yogurt for extra protein.

Nutrition per serving: Calories: 220 | Protein: 8g | Carbohydrates: 25g | Fiber: 8g | Fat: 11g | Cholesterol: 0mg | Sodium: 280mg | Potassium: 500mg

Warm Mushroom and Spinach Salad

Prep. time: 10 min | **Cook time:** 10 min | **Servings:** 4

Ingredients:

- 8 oz mushrooms, sliced
- 6 cups fresh spinach
- 1/4 red onion, thinly sliced
- 2 tbsp olive oil
- 1 tsp garlic powder
- 1/4 cup walnuts, chopped
- 2 oz goat cheese, crumbled
- Salt and pepper to taste

Dressing:

- 2 tbsp balsamic vinegar
- 1 tbsp olive oil
- 1 tsp Dijon mustard
- 1 small garlic clove, minced

Directions:

1. Toss mushrooms with 1 tbsp olive oil, garlic powder, salt, and pepper.
2. Preheat air fryer to 380°F (193°C).
3. Air fry mushrooms for 8-10 minutes, shaking basket halfway through.
4. Arrange spinach and onion on plates.
5. Top with warm mushrooms, walnuts, and goat cheese.
6. Whisk dressing ingredients and drizzle over salad.

Serving suggestion: Add grilled chicken breast for extra protein.

Nutrition per serving: Calories: 220 | Protein: 7g | Carbohydrates: 8g | Fiber: 3g | Fat: 19g | Cholesterol: 7mg | Sodium: 150mg | Potassium: 550mg

Pear and Walnut Winter Salad

Prep. time: 10 min | **Cook time:** 10 min | **Servings:** 4

Ingredients:

- 2 medium pears, cored and sliced
- 6 cups mixed winter greens (e.g., kale, arugula, spinach)
- 1/2 cup walnuts, roughly chopped
- 2 oz blue cheese, crumbled
- 1 tbsp olive oil
- 1 tsp cinnamon
- 1 tsp erythritol or stevia blend

Dressing:

- 2 tbsp apple cider vinegar
- 1 tbsp olive oil
- 1 tsp Dijon mustard

Directions:

1. Toss pear slices with 1 tbsp olive oil, cinnamon, and sweetener.
2. Preheat the air fryer to 350°F (175°C).
3. Air fry pears for 8-10 minutes, shaking basket halfway through.
4. Arrange greens on plates.
5. Top with warm pears, walnuts, and blue cheese.
6. Whisk dressing ingredients and drizzle over salad.

Serving suggestion: Add grilled chicken or turkey for extra protein.

Nutrition per serving: Calories: 250 | Protein: 6g | Carbohydrates: 20g | Fiber: 5g | Fat: 18g | Cholesterol: 8mg | Sodium: 200mg | Potassium: 300mg

Beetroot and Feta Salad

Prep. time: 15 min **Cook time:** 20 min **Servings:** 4

Ingredients:

- 4 medium beetroots, peeled and cubed
- 6 cups mixed salad greens
- 2 oz feta cheese, crumbled
- 1/4 cup walnuts, chopped
- 1 tbsp olive oil
- 1 tsp dried thyme
- Salt and pepper to taste

Dressing:

- 2 tbsp balsamic vinegar
- 1 tbsp olive oil
- 1 tsp Dijon mustard
- 1 small garlic clove, minced

Directions:

1. Toss beetroot cubes with 1 tbsp olive oil, thyme, salt, and pepper.
2. Preheat the air fryer to 380°F (193°C).
3. Air fry beetroots for 18-20 minutes, shaking basket every 5 minutes.
4. Arrange salad greens on plates.
5. Top with warm beetroots, feta, and walnuts.
6. Whisk dressing ingredients and drizzle over salad.

Serving suggestion: Add grilled chicken or chickpeas for extra protein.

Nutrition per serving: Calories: 200 | Protein: 6g | Carbohydrates: 15g | Fiber: 4g | Fat: 14g | Cholesterol: 11mg | Sodium: 250mg | Potassium: 450mg

Warm Halloumi and Tomato Salad

Prep. time: 10 min **Cook time:** 8 min **Servings:** 4

Ingredients:

- 8 oz halloumi cheese, sliced
- 2 cups cherry tomatoes
- 6 cups mixed salad greens
- 1/4 cup fresh basil leaves, torn
- 1 tbsp olive oil
- 1 tsp dried oregano
- 1/4 cup pine nuts

Dressing:

- 2 tbsp balsamic vinegar
- 1 tbsp olive oil
- 1 tsp Dijon mustard
- 1 small garlic clove, minced

Directions:

1. Toss halloumi and tomatoes with 1 tbsp olive oil and oregano.
2. Preheat the air fryer to 375°F (190°C).
3. Air fry halloumi and tomatoes for 6-8 minutes, shaking basket halfway.
4. Arrange salad greens on plates.
5. Top with warm halloumi, tomatoes, basil, and pine nuts.
6. Whisk dressing ingredients and drizzle over salad.

Serving suggestion: Add grilled chicken for extra protein if desired.

Nutrition per serving: Calories: 260 | Protein: 12g | Carbohydrates: 8g | Fiber: 3g | Fat: 21g | Cholesterol: 25mg | Sodium: 380mg | Potassium: 300mg

Sides

Air-Fried Green Beans Almondine

Prep. time: 10 min | Cook time: 12 min | Servings: 4

Ingredients:

- 1 lb fresh green beans, trimmed
- 1/4 cup sliced almonds
- 1 tbsp olive oil
- 1 clove garlic, minced
- 1 tsp lemon zest
- Salt and pepper to taste

Directions:

1. Preheat the air fryer to 380°F (193°C).
2. Toss green beans with olive oil, garlic, salt, and pepper in a bowl.
3. Place green beans in an air fryer basket. Cook for 8-10 minutes, shaking basket halfway through, until tender-crisp.
4. Add sliced almonds to the basket for the last 2 minutes of cooking.
5. Transfer to a serving bowl and toss with lemon zest.

Serving suggestion: Serve immediately as a side dish. Squeeze fresh lemon juice over the top if desired.

Nutritional Information (per serving): Calories: 110 | Protein: 4g | Carbohydrates: 9g | Fiber: 4g | Sugar: 3g | Fat: 8g (mostly healthy fats) | Cholesterol: 0mg | Sodium: 50mg | Potassium: 230mg

Lemon-Pepper Asparagus Spears

Prep. time: 5 min | Cook time: 8 min | Servings: 4

Ingredients:

- 1 lb fresh asparagus spears, trimmed
- 1 tbsp olive oil
- 1 tsp lemon zest
- 1 tsp freshly ground black pepper
- 1/4 tsp garlic powder
- Salt to taste

Directions:

1. Preheat the air fryer to 400°F (200°C).
2. In a bowl, toss asparagus with olive oil, lemon zest, black pepper, garlic powder, and salt.
3. Arrange asparagus in an air fryer basket in a single layer. You may need to cook in batches.
4. Cook for 6-8 minutes, shaking basket halfway through, until tender-crisp and lightly charred.

Serving suggestion: Serve immediately. Squeeze fresh lemon juice over the asparagus just before serving for extra flavor.

Nutritional Information (per serving): Calories: 60 | Protein: 3g | Carbohydrates: 5g | Fiber: 3g | Sugar: 2g | Fat: 4g (mostly healthy fats) | Cholesterol: 0mg | Sodium: 30mg | Potassium: 230mg

Cauliflower Mac' and Cheese

Prep. time: 10 min **Cook time:** 15 min **Servings:** 4

Ingredients:

- 1 large head cauliflower, cut into florets
- 1 cup shredded cheddar cheese
- 1/4 cup grated Parmesan cheese
- 1/4 cup unsweetened almond milk
- 1 egg
- 1 tsp Dijon mustard
- 1/4 tsp garlic powder
- 1/4 tsp onion powder
- Salt and pepper to taste
- 2 tbsp almond flour (for topping)

Directions:

1. Preheat the air fryer to 375°F (190°C).
2. Steam cauliflower florets until just tender, about 5 minutes. Drain well.
3. Mix cheddar, Parmesan, almond milk, egg, mustard, garlic powder, onion powder, salt, and pepper in a bowl.
4. Gently fold the cauliflower into the cheese mixture.
5. Transfer to an air fryer-safe dish that fits in your basket.
6. Sprinkle almond flour on top.
7. Air fry for 10-12 minutes until golden and bubbly.

Serving suggestion: Serve hot, garnished with fresh parsley if desired.

Nutritional Information (per serving): Calories: 220 | Protein: 15g | Carbohydrates: 8g | Fiber: 3g | Sugar: 3g | Fat: 16g (mostly from cheese) | Cholesterol: 70mg | Sodium: 350mg | Potassium: 450mg

Chicken Bruschetta

Prep. time: 15 min **Cook time:** 152min **Servings:** 4

Ingredients:

- 2 medium zucchinis
- 1/2 cup grated Parmesan cheese
- 1/4 cup almond flour
- 1 tsp garlic powder
- 1 tsp dried oregano
- 1/4 tsp salt
- 1/4 tsp black pepper
- 1 large egg, beaten

Directions:

1. Preheat the air fryer to 400°F (200°C).
2. Cut zucchini into 1/2-inch-thick sticks.
3. Mix Parmesan, almond flour, garlic powder, oregano, salt, and pepper in a shallow bowl.
4. Dip zucchini sticks in beaten egg, then coat with Parmesan mixture.
5. Place coated zucchini in an air fryer basket in a single layer, working in batches if needed.
6. Cook for 10-12 minutes, shaking basket halfway through, until golden and crispy.

Serving suggestion: Serve hot with sugar-free marinara sauce or Greek yogurt dip.

Nutritional Information (per serving): Calories: 140 |Protein: 10g | Carbohydrates: 6g | Fiber: 2g | Sugar: 2g | Fat: 9g (mostly from cheese and almond flour) | Cholesterol: 60mg | Sodium: 330mg | Potassium: 300mg

Spicy Okra with Cool Yogurt Dip

Prep. time: 15 min   **Cook time:** 15 min   **Servings:** 4

Ingredients:

For the Spicy Okra:
- 1-pound fresh okra, trimmed and sliced lengthwise
- 1 tablespoon olive oil
- 1 teaspoon smoked paprika
- 1/2 teaspoon cayenne pepper
- 1/2 teaspoon garlic powder
- 1/4 teaspoon salt
- 1/4 teaspoon black pepper

For the Cool Yogurt Dip:
- 1 cup plain Greek yogurt
- 1 tablespoon fresh lemon juice
- 1 small cucumber, finely diced
- 1 tablespoon fresh mint, chopped
- 1 clove garlic, minced
- Salt and pepper to taste

Directions:

1. Preheat the air fryer to 375°F (190°C).
2. In a large bowl, toss the okra with olive oil, paprika, cayenne, garlic powder, salt, and pepper.
3. Place okra in an air fryer basket in a single layer, working in batches if necessary.
4. Cook for 12-15 minutes, shaking the basket every 5 minutes for even cooking.
5. While okra is cooking, prepare the yogurt dip. Mix all dip ingredients in a bowl and refrigerate until ready to serve.
6. Remove the okra from the air fryer once it is crispy and lightly browned.
7. Serve hot okra immediately with chilled yogurt dip on the side.

Nutritional Information (per serving): Calories: 120 | Protein: 8g | Carbohydrates: 12g | Fiber: 5g | Fat: 6g | Cholesterol: 5mg | Sodium: 180mg | Potassium: 450mg

Crispy Brussels Sprouts with Balsamic Glaze

Prep. time: 10 min   **Cook time:** 15 min   **Servings:** 4

Ingredients:

For the Brussels Sprouts

- 1 pound Brussels sprouts, trimmed and halved
- 1 tablespoon olive oil
- 1/4 teaspoon salt
- 1/4 teaspoon black pepper

For the Balsamic Glaze:

- 2 tablespoons balsamic vinegar
- 1 teaspoon Dijon mustard
- 1 teaspoon erythritol or stevia
- 1 clove garlic, minced

Directions:

1. Preheat the air fryer to 375°F (190°C).
2. Toss Brussels sprouts with olive oil, salt, and pepper in a bowl.
3. Place sprouts in an air fryer basket in a single layer.
4. Cook for 12-15 minutes, shaking basket every 5 minutes for even cooking.
5. Whisk balsamic glaze ingredients in a small bowl while sprouts cook.
6. Transfer to a serving bowl Once sprouts are crispy and browned.
7. Drizzle with balsamic glaze and toss to coat.
8. Serve immediately.

Nutritional Information (per serving): Calories: 95 | Protein: 4g | Carbohydrates: 11g | Fiber: 4g | Fat: 5g | Cholesterol: 0mg | Sodium: 170mg | Potassium: 450mg

Garlic & Rosemary Roasted Turnips

Prep. time: 10 min   **Cook time:** 20 min   **Servings:** 4

Ingredients:

- 1-pound turnips, peeled and cut into 1-inch cubes
- 2 tablespoons olive oil
- 3 cloves garlic, minced
- 1 tablespoon fresh rosemary, chopped
- 1/2 teaspoon salt
- 1/4 teaspoon black pepper
- 1 tablespoon grated Parmesan cheese (optional)

Directions:

1. Preheat the air fryer to 400°F (200°C).
2. In a bowl, toss turnip cubes with olive oil, garlic, rosemary, salt, and pepper.
3. Place seasoned turnips in an air fryer basket in a single layer.
4. Cook for 15 minutes, shaking basket halfway through.
5. Check for doneness. If needed, cook for 3-5 minutes until golden and crispy.
6. Optional: Sprinkle with Parmesan cheese before serving.

Serving suggestion: Serve as a side dish with lean protein and non-starchy vegetables.

Nutritional Information (per serving): Calories: 90 | Protein: 1g | Carbohydrates: 8g | Fiber: 2g | Fat: 7g | Cholesterol: 0mg | Sodium: 330mg | Potassium: 230mg

Cauliflower Rice Pilaf with Carrots and Peas

Prep. time: 15 min   **Cook time:** 15 min   **Servings:** 4

Ingredients:

- 1 medium cauliflower, riced (about 4 cups)
- 1 cup carrots, diced small
- 1/2 cup frozen peas
- 2 tablespoons olive oil
- 1 small onion, finely chopped
- 2 cloves garlic, minced
- 1 teaspoon cumin
- 1/2 teaspoon turmeric
- 1/4 cup low-sodium vegetable broth
- Salt and pepper to taste
- 2 tablespoons fresh parsley, chopped

Directions:

1. Preheat the air fryer to 375°F (190°C).
2. Mix cauliflower rice, carrots, onion, garlic, olive oil, cumin, and turmeric in a large bowl.
3. Transfer the mixture to the air fryer basket. Cook for 10 minutes, shaking basket every 3-4 minutes.
4. Add peas and vegetable broth. Cook for an additional 5 minutes.
5. Season with salt and pepper. Stir in fresh parsley before serving.

Serving suggestion: Serve as a side dish, or add grilled chicken or tofu for a complete meal.

Nutritional Information (per serving): Calories: 120 | Protein: 4g | Carbohydrates: 14g | Fiber: 5g | Fat: 7g | Cholesterol: 0mg | Sodium: 80mg | Potassium: 450mg

Sesame Ginger Broccoli Stir-fry

Prep. time: 10 min | Cook time: 10 min | Servings: 4

Ingredients:

- 4 cups broccoli florets
- 1 red bell pepper, sliced
- 1 tablespoon sesame oil
- 2 cloves garlic, minced
- 1 tablespoon fresh ginger, grated
- 2 tablespoons low-sodium soy sauce
- 1 tablespoon rice vinegar
- 1 teaspoon monk fruit sweetener
- 1 tablespoon sesame seeds
- 1/4 cup green onions, chopped

Directions:

1. Preheat the air fryer to 375°F (190°C).
2. Toss broccoli and bell pepper with sesame oil, garlic, and ginger in a bowl.
3. Air fry for 8 minutes, shaking basket halfway through.
4. Mix soy sauce, rice vinegar, and monk fruit sweetener in a small bowl.
5. Pour sauce over the vegetables in the basket. Air fry for 2 more minutes.
6. Sprinkle with sesame seeds and green onions before serving.

Serving suggestion: Pair with grilled tofu or lean protein for a complete meal.

Nutritional Information (per serving): Calories: 85 | Protein: 4g | Carbohydrates: 10g | Fiber: 3g | Fat: 4g | Cholesterol: 0mg | Sodium: 280mg | Potassium: 350mg

Italian Herb Roasted Bell Peppers

Prep. time: 10 min | Cook time: 15 min | Servings: 4

Ingredients:

- 4 medium bell peppers, mixed colors, sliced
- 2 tablespoons olive oil
- 2 cloves garlic, minced
- 1 teaspoon dried oregano
- 1 teaspoon dried basil
- 1/2 teaspoon dried thyme
- 1/4 teaspoon red pepper flakes (optional)
- Salt and black pepper to taste
- 1 tablespoon balsamic vinegar
- 1 tablespoon fresh parsley, chopped

Directions:

1. Preheat the air fryer to 380°F (193°C).
2. In a bowl, toss sliced peppers with olive oil, garlic, oregano, basil, thyme, red pepper flakes, salt, and black pepper.
3. Place seasoned peppers in the air fryer basket in a single layer.
4. Cook for 12-15 minutes, shaking the basket every 5 minutes.
5. Transfer to a serving bowl once peppers are tender and slightly charred.
6. Drizzle with balsamic vinegar and sprinkle with fresh parsley before serving.

Serving suggestion: Serve as a side dish with grilled lean protein or add to a salad.

Nutritional Information (per serving): Calories: 95 | Protein: 1g | Carbohydrates: 8g | Fiber: 2g | Fat: 7g | Cholesterol: 0mg | Sodium: 5mg (without added salt) | Potassium: 230mg

Italian Baked Eggplant Sticks with Marinara Dip

Prep. time: 15 min **Cook time:** 15 min **Servings:** 4

Ingredients:

For the eggplant sticks:
- 1 large eggplant, cut into 1/2-inch-thick sticks
- 1/4 cup almond flour
- 1/4 cup grated Parmesan cheese
- 1 tsp dried Italian herbs
- 1/4 tsp garlic powder
- 1/4 tsp salt
- 1/8 tsp black pepper
- 1 large egg, beaten
- Olive oil spray

For the marinara dip:
- 1/2 cup low-sugar marinara sauce
- 1 tsp olive oil
- 1/4 tsp dried basil

Directions:

1. Preheat the air fryer to 400°F (200°C).
2. Mix almond flour, Parmesan, Italian herbs, garlic powder, salt, and pepper in a shallow dish.
3. Dip eggplant sticks in beaten egg, then coat with almond flour.
4. Place coated sticks in the air fryer basket in a single layer. Spray lightly with olive oil.
5. Cook for 12-15 minutes, turning halfway through, until golden and crispy.
6. Meanwhile, mix marinara sauce ingredients in a small bowl.
7. Serve eggplant sticks hot with marinara dip on the side.

Serving suggestion: Serve with a side salad for a complete meal.

Nutritional Information (per serving): Calories: 150 | Protein: 8g | Carbohydrates: 12g | Fiber: 5g | Fat: 9g | Cholesterol: 55mg | Sodium: 380mg | Potassium: 450mg

Sweet & Savory Butternut Squash Wedges

Prep. time: 15 min **Cook time:** 20 min **Servings:** 4

Ingredients:

- 1 medium butternut squash (about 2 lbs), peeled and cut into 1-inch wedges
- 2 tablespoons olive oil
- 1 tablespoon sugar-free maple syrup
- 1 teaspoon cinnamon
- 1/2 teaspoon dried thyme
- 1/4 teaspoon salt
- 1/8 teaspoon black pepper
- 1 tablespoon pumpkin seeds (optional)

Directions:

1. Preheat the air fryer to 375°F (190°C).
2. In a large bowl, toss squash wedges with olive oil, sugar-free maple syrup, cinnamon, thyme, salt, and pepper.
3. Arrange seasoned squash in the air fryer basket in a single layer. You may need to cook in batches.
4. Air fry for 15-20 minutes, shaking the basket or flipping wedges halfway through.
5. If desired, sprinkle pumpkin seeds over squash for the last 2 minutes of cooking.
6. Squash is done when tender and lightly caramelized.

Serving suggestion: Serve as a side dish or add to a salad for a more substantial meal.

Nutritional Information (per serving): Calories: 140 | Protein: 2g | Carbohydrates: 20g | Fiber: 3g | Fat: 7g | Cholesterol: 0mg | Sodium: 150mg | Potassium: 450mg

Fresh Herbs and Lemon Green Beans

Prep. time: 5 min   **Cook time:** 8 min   **Servings:** 4

Ingredients:

- 1-pound fresh green beans, trimmed
- 1 tablespoon olive oil
- 1 lemon, zested and juiced
- 2 cloves garlic, minced
- 1 tablespoon fresh parsley, chopped
- 1 tablespoon fresh basil, chopped
- 1/4 teaspoon salt
- 1/8 teaspoon black pepper
- 2 tablespoons sliced almonds (optional)

Directions:

Instructions:

1. Preheat the air fryer to 380°F (193°C).
2. Toss green beans with olive oil, lemon zest, garlic, salt, and pepper in a bowl.
3. Place beans in the air fryer basket in a single layer.
4. Cook for 6-8 minutes, shaking the basket halfway through.
5. Transfer beans to a serving bowl and toss with lemon juice, parsley, and basil.
6. If using, sprinkle with sliced almonds before serving.

Serving suggestion: Pair with grilled lean protein for a complete meal.

Nutritional Information (per serving): Calories: 75 | Protein: 2g | Carbohydrates: 8g | Fiber: 3g | Fat: 4g | Cholesterol: 0mg | Sodium: 150mg | Potassium: 230mg

Mediterranean Spiced Air Fryer Chickpeas

Prep. time: 5 min   **Cook time:** 15 min   **Servings:** 4

Ingredients:

- 1 can (15 oz) chickpeas, drained and rinsed
- 1 tablespoon olive oil
- 1 teaspoon smoked paprika
- 1/2 teaspoon ground cumin
- 1/2 teaspoon dried oregano
- 1/4 teaspoon garlic powder
- 1/4 teaspoon salt
- 1/8 teaspoon black pepper
- Zest of 1 lemon

Directions:

1. Preheat the air fryer to 390°F (200°C).
2. Pat chickpeas dry with paper towels.
3. Toss chickpeas with olive oil and all spices except lemon zest in a bowl.
4. Spread chickpeas in an air fryer basket in a single layer.
5. Cook for 12-15 minutes, shaking basket every 5 minutes.
6. Remove when crispy and golden. Toss with lemon zest.

Serving suggestion: Enjoy as a snack or add to salads for extra protein and crunch.

Nutritional Information (per serving): Calories: 120 | Protein: 5g | Carbohydrates: 15g | Fiber: 4g | Fat: 5g | Cholesterol: 0mg | Sodium: 240mg | Potassium: 170mg

Stuffed Mushroom Caps with Spinach and Ricotta

Prep. time: 15 min   **Cook time:** 12 min   **Servings:** 4

Ingredients:

- 16 medium-sized mushrooms, stems removed
- 1 cup fresh spinach, chopped
- 1/2 cup part-skim ricotta cheese
- 2 tablespoons grated Parmesan cheese
- 1 clove garlic, minced
- 1/4 teaspoon dried oregano
- 1/8 teaspoon black pepper
- 1 tablespoon olive oil
- 1 tablespoon fresh parsley, chopped

Directions:

1. Preheat the air fryer to 375°F (190°C).
2. Mix spinach, ricotta, Parmesan, garlic, oregano, and pepper in a bowl.
3. Brush mushroom caps with olive oil.
4. Fill each cap with the spinach-ricotta mixture.
5. Place stuffed mushrooms in the air fryer basket in a single layer.
6. Cook for 10-12 minutes until mushrooms are tender and the filling is hot.
7. Sprinkle with fresh parsley before serving.

Serving suggestion: Serve as an appetizer or side dish with a lean protein main course.

Nutritional Information (per serving - 4 stuffed mushrooms): Calories: 120 | Protein: 8g | Carbohydrates: 5g | Fiber: 1g | Fat: 8g | Cholesterol: 15mg | Sodium: 120mg | Potassium: 350mg

Garlic-Parmesan Air Fryer Brussels Sprouts

Prep. time: 10 min   **Cook time:** 15 min   **Servings:** 4

Ingredients:

- 1 lb Brussels sprouts, trimmed and halved
- 2 tbsp olive oil
- 3 cloves garlic, minced
- 1/4 cup grated Parmesan cheese
- 1/4 tsp salt
- 1/4 tsp black pepper
- 1 tbsp lemon juice

Directions:

1. Toss Brussels sprouts in a bowl with olive oil, garlic, salt, and pepper.
2. Preheat air fryer to 380°F (193°C).
3. Place Brussels sprouts in the air fryer basket in a single layer.
4. Cook for 10 minutes, shaking the basket halfway through.
5. Sprinkle Parmesan cheese over the sprouts.
6. Cook for 2-5 minutes until crispy and golden brown.
7. Drizzle with lemon juice before serving.

Serving suggestion: Pair with grilled lean protein for a complete meal.

Nutrition per serving: Calories: 140 | Protein: 6g | Carbohydrates: 10g | Fiber: 4g | Fat: 10g | Cholesterol: 5mg | Sodium: 230mg | Potassium: 450mg

Soups

Creamy Broccoli Soup with Air-Fryer Croutons

Prep. time: 15 min **Cook time:** 25 min **Servings:** 4

Ingredients:

- 4 cups broccoli florets
- 1 medium onion, chopped
- 2 cloves garlic, minced
- 3 cups low-sodium vegetable broth
- 1/2 cup unsweetened almond milk
- 1/4 cup Greek yogurt
- 1 tbsp olive oil
- 1 tsp dried thyme
- Salt and pepper to taste

- 2 slices whole grain bread, cubed
- 1 tbsp olive oil
- 1/4 tsp garlic powder
- 1/4 tsp dried oregano

Directions:

1. Preheat the air fryer to 375°F (190°C).
2. In a pot, sauté onion and garlic in olive oil until soft.
3. Add broccoli, broth, and thyme. Simmer for 15 minutes.
4. Meanwhile, toss bread cubes with oil and seasonings.
5. Air fry croutons for 5-7 minutes, shaking halfway through.
6. Blend soup until smooth. Stir in almond milk and yogurt.
7. Season with salt and pepper.
8. Serve soup topped with air-fried croutons.

Serving suggestion: Pair with a side salad for a complete meal.

Nutritional Information (per serving): Calories: 180 | Protein: 8g | Carbohydrates: 20g | Fiber: 5g | Fat: 10g | Cholesterol: 2mg | Sodium: 180mg | Potassium: 450mg

Low-Carb Tomato Basil Soup with Parmesan Crisps

Prep. time: 10 min **Cook time:** 25 min **Servings:** 4

Ingredients:

For the soup:
- 2 cans (14.5 oz each) diced tomatoes, no added sugar
- 1 medium onion, chopped
- 2 cloves garlic, minced
- 2 cups low-sodium vegetable broth
- 1/4 cup heavy cream
- 1/4 cup fresh basil leaves, chopped
- 1 tbsp olive oil
- 1 tsp erythritol (optional for sweetness)
- Salt and pepper to taste

For the Parmesan crisps:
- 1 cup grated Parmesan cheese

Directions:

1. In a pot, sauté onion and garlic in olive oil until soft.
2. Add tomatoes, broth, and erythritol. Simmer for 15 minutes.
3. Blend soup until smooth. Stir in cream and basil.
4. Preheat the air fryer to 400°F (200°C).
5. For Parmesan crisps: Place 1 tbsp mounds of cheese on parchment paper in the air fryer basket.
6. Air fry for 3-4 minutes until golden and crisp.
7. Let crisps cool for 1 minute before removing.
8. Serve soup hot with Parmesan crisps on top.

Serving suggestion: Pair with a side of mixed greens for added nutrients.

Nutritional Information (per serving): Calories: 220 | Protein: 11g | Carbohydrates: 12g | Fiber: 3g | Fat: 16g | Cholesterol: 35mg | Sodium: 480mg | Potassium: 550mg

Spicy Chicken & Veggie Soup with Tortilla Strips

Ingredients:

Prep. time: 15 min | **Cook time:** 30 min | **Servings:** 4

For the soup:
- 1 lb boneless, skinless chicken breast, diced
- 1 medium onion, chopped
- 2 cloves garlic, minced
- 1 red bell pepper, diced
- 1 cup zucchini, diced
- 1 can (14.5 oz) diced tomatoes, no added sugar
- 4 cups low-sodium chicken broth
- 1 tbsp olive oil
- 1 tsp ground cumin
- 1 tsp chili powder
- 1/4 tsp cayenne pepper (adjust to taste)
- Salt and pepper to taste

For the tortilla strips:
- 2 small low-carb tortillas, cut into strips
- 1 tsp olive oil
- 1/4 tsp salt

Directions:

1. In a pot, sauté chicken, onion, and garlic in olive oil until chicken is cooked.
2. Add bell pepper, zucchini, tomatoes, broth, and spices. Simmer for 20 minutes.
3. Preheat the air fryer to 375°F (190°C).
4. Toss tortilla strips with oil and salt.
5. Air fry strips for 3-5 minutes, shaking halfway through, until crispy.
6. Serve soup hot, topped with air-fried tortilla strips.

Serving suggestion: Garnish with fresh cilantro and a dollop of Greek yogurt if desired.

Nutritional Information (per serving): Calories: 250 | Protein: 28g | Carbohydrates: 15g | Fiber: 4g | Fat: 10g | Cholesterol: 65mg | Sodium: 480mg | Potassium: 720mg

Vegetable Barley Soup

Prep. time: 15 min | **Cook time:** 40 min | **Servings:** 4

Ingredients:

- 1/2 cup pearl barley
- 4 cups low-sodium vegetable broth
- 1 medium onion, diced
- 2 cloves garlic, minced
- 1 can (14.5 oz) diced tomatoes, no added sugar
- 1 tbsp olive oil
- 1 tsp dried thyme
- 1 bay leaf
- Salt and pepper to taste

- 1 cup carrots, chopped
- 1 cup zucchini, chopped
- 1 cup bell peppers, chopped
- 1 tbsp olive oil
- 1/2 tsp garlic powder
- 1/4 tsp smoked paprika

Directions:

1. In a pot, sauté onion and garlic in olive oil until soft.
2. Add barley, broth, tomatoes, thyme, and bay leaf. Simmer for 30 minutes.
3. Preheat the air fryer to 400°F (200°C).
4. Toss chopped vegetables with oil, garlic powder, and paprika.
5. Air fry vegetables for 10-12 minutes, shaking basket halfway through.
6. Remove the bay leaf from the soup. Add air-fried vegetables to the soup.
7. Simmer for an additional 5 minutes. Season with salt and pepper.

Serving suggestion: Garnish with fresh parsley and a sprinkle of Parmesan cheese if desired.

Nutritional Information (per serving): Calories: 220 | Protein: 6g | Carbohydrates: 35g | Fiber: 8g | Fat: 8g | Cholesterol: 0mg | Sodium: 280mg | Potassium: 620mg

Cauliflower & Cheddar Cheese Soup

Prep. time: 15 min | **Cook time:** 30 min | **Servings:** 4

Ingredients:

For the soup:
- 1 large head cauliflower, cut into florets
- 1 medium onion, chopped
- 2 cloves garlic, minced
- 4 cups low-sodium vegetable broth
- 1 cup unsweetened almond milk
- 1 cup sharp cheddar cheese, shredded
- 1 tbsp olive oil
- 1 tsp dried thyme
- Salt and pepper to taste

For cauliflower croutons:
- 1 cup small cauliflower florets
- 1 tbsp olive oil
- 1/4 tsp garlic powder
- 1/4 tsp smoked paprika

Directions:

1. Preheat the air fryer to 400°F (200°C).
2. Toss 1 cup cauliflower florets with oil, garlic powder, and paprika.
3. Air fry for 10-12 minutes, shaking basket halfway through, until crispy.
4. In a pot, sauté onion and garlic in olive oil until soft.
5. Add remaining cauliflower, broth, and thyme. Simmer for 15 minutes.
6. Blend soup until smooth. Stir in almond milk and cheese until melted.
7. Season with salt and pepper.
8. Serve soup topped with air-fried cauliflower croutons.

Serving suggestion: Garnish with fresh chives or a sprinkle of extra cheddar.

Nutritional Information (per serving): Calories: 220 | Protein: 12g | Carbohydrates: 14g | Fiber: 5g | Fat: 15g | Cholesterol: 20mg | Sodium: 380mg | Potassium: 620mg

Roasted Red Pepper Gazpacho

Prep. time: 15 min | **Cook time:** 15 min | **Servings:** 4

Ingredients:

- 3 large red bell peppers
- 2 medium tomatoes
- 1 cucumber, peeled and chopped
- 1/4 red onion, chopped
- 2 cloves garlic
- 2 tbsp olive oil
- 2 tbsp red wine vinegar
- 1 tsp smoked paprika
- Salt and pepper to taste

- 1 medium zucchini, thinly sliced
- 1 tbsp olive oil
- 1/4 tsp garlic powder
- 1/4 tsp sea salt

Directions:

1. Preheat the air fryer to 400°F (200°C).
2. Halve and deseed bell peppers. Air fry for 10-12 minutes until skin is charred.
3. Place peppers in a bowl and cover with plastic wrap to steam for 5 minutes.
4. Peel off the skin from the peppers once cooled.
5. Blend roasted peppers, tomatoes, cucumber, onion, garlic, olive oil, vinegar, and paprika until smooth.
6. Chill gazpacho for at least 2 hours.
7. Toss zucchini slices with oil, garlic powder, and salt for vegetable chips.
8. Air fry at 375°F (190°C) for 10-12 minutes, shaking basket halfway through, until crispy.
9. Serve chilled gazpacho with air-fried zucchini chips.

Serving suggestion: Chilling time: 2 hours. Garnish with a dollop of Greek yogurt and fresh basil.

Nutritional Information (per serving): Calories: 150 | Protein: 3g | Carbohydrates: 15g | Fiber: 4g | Fat: 10g | Cholesterol: 0mg | Sodium: 180mg | Potassium: 520mg

Roasted Pumpkin Bisque with Greek Yogurt Swirl

Prep. time: 15 min | **Cook time:** 30 min | **Servings:** 4

Ingredients:

- 4 cups pumpkin, cubed
- 1 medium onion, chopped
- 2 cloves garlic, minced
- 3 cups low-sodium vegetable broth
- 1/2 cup unsweetened almond milk
- 1 tbsp olive oil
- 1 tsp ground cinnamon
- 1/4 tsp ground nutmeg
- Salt and pepper to taste

- 1/2 cup Greek yogurt
- 1 tsp lemon juice
- 1 tbsp pumpkin seeds

Directions:

1. Preheat the air fryer to 400°F (200°C).
2. Toss pumpkin cubes with 1/2 tbsp olive oil, salt, and pepper.
3. Air fry pumpkin for 15-20 minutes, shaking basket halfway through, until tender.
4. In a pot, sauté onion and garlic in the remaining olive oil until soft.
5. Add roasted pumpkin, broth, almond milk, cinnamon, and nutmeg. Simmer for 10 minutes.
6. Blend soup until smooth. Season with salt and pepper.
7. Mix Greek yogurt with lemon juice.
8. Air fry pumpkin seeds at 350°F (175°C) for 3-5 minutes until toasted.
9. Serve bisque with a swirl of yogurt mixture and toasted pumpkin seeds.

Serving suggestion: Pair with a small side salad of mixed greens.

Nutritional Information (per serving): Calories: 180 | Protein: 7g | Carbohydrates: 25g | Fiber: 6g | Fat: 8g | Cholesterol: 2mg | Sodium: 220mg | Potassium: 580mg

Creamy Mushroom Soup with Thyme

Prep. time: 15 min | **Cook time:** 20 min | **Servings:** 4

Ingredients:

- 1 lb mixed mushrooms, sliced
- 1 medium onion, chopped
- 2 cloves garlic, minced
- 4 cups low-sodium vegetable broth
- 1/2 cup unsweetened almond milk
- 1/4 cup heavy cream
- 2 tbsp olive oil
- 1 tbsp fresh thyme leaves
- Salt and pepper to taste

- 1 cup thinly sliced mushrooms
- 1 tsp olive oil
- 1/4 tsp garlic powder
- 1/8 tsp salt

Directions:

1. Preheat the air fryer to 375°F (190°C).
2. Toss 1 cup sliced mushrooms with 1 tsp oil, garlic powder, and salt.
3. Air fry for 8-10 minutes, shaking basket halfway through, until crispy.
4. In a pot, sauté onion and garlic in 1 tbsp olive oil until soft.
5. Add remaining mushrooms and thyme and cook for 5 minutes.
6. Add broth, simmer for 15 minutes.
7. Blend soup until smooth. Stir in almond milk and cream.
8. Season with salt and pepper.
9. Serve soup topped with air-fried mushroom chips.

Serving suggestion: Garnish with additional fresh thyme leaves.

Nutritional Information (per serving): Calories: 180 | Protein: 5g | Carbohydrates: 12g | Fiber: 3g | Fat: 13g | Cholesterol: 15mg | Sodium: 250mg | Potassium: 550mg

Chicken Zoodle Pro

Prep. time: 20 min **Cook time:** 15 min **Servings:** 4

Ingredients:

- 1 lb boneless, skinless chicken breast, cubed
- 4 medium zucchinis, spiralized
- 1 tbsp olive oil
- 2 tsp Italian seasoning
- 1/2 tsp garlic powder
- 1/4 tsp salt
- 1/4 tsp black pepper
- 1/4 cup grated Parmesan cheese
- 1 tbsp lemon juice
- 2 tbsp chopped fresh basil

Directions:

1. In a bowl, toss cubed chicken with olive oil, Italian seasoning, garlic powder, salt, and pepper.
2. Preheat air fryer to 380°F (193°C).
3. Place seasoned chicken in the air fryer basket in a single layer. Cook for 11-12 minutes, shaking the basket halfway through.
4. While chicken cooks, spiralize zucchini into "zoodles."
5. Once the chicken is done, remove it from the air fryer and set it aside.
6. Place zoodles in the air fryer basket. Cook for 3-4 minutes at 380°F (193°C), shaking halfway through.
7. Combine cooked chicken and zoodles in a large bowl. Toss with Parmesan cheese, lemon juice, and fresh basil.

Serving suggestion: Divide into four portions and serve immediately.

Nutritional Information (per serving): Calories: 245 | Protein: 32g | Carbohydrates: 8g | Fiber: 2g | Fat: 10g | Cholesterol: 85mg | Sodium: 380mg | Potassium: 750mg

Hearty Turkey and Bean Chili Soup

Prep. time: 15 min **Cook time:** 30 min **Servings:** 4

Ingredients:

- 1 lb lean ground turkey
- 1 medium onion, diced
- 2 bell peppers, diced
- 2 cloves garlic, minced
- 1 can (14.5 oz) low-sodium diced tomatoes
- 1 can (15 oz) black beans, drained and rinsed
- 2 cups low-sodium chicken broth
- 2 tbsp chili powder
- 1 tsp ground cumin
- 1 tsp dried oregano
- 1/4 tsp cayenne pepper (optional)
- Salt and pepper to taste
- 2 tbsp olive oil

Directions:

1. Preheat the air fryer to 375°F (190°C).
2. Mix ground turkey with 1 tbsp chili powder, cumin, oregano, salt, and pepper in a bowl.
3. Place the turkey mixture into small meatballs in an air fryer basket. Cook for 8-10 minutes, shaking basket halfway through.
4. While the meatballs cook, combine the onion, peppers, and garlic with 1 tablespoon olive oil in a bowl.
5. Remove the meatballs and set aside. Add the vegetable mixture to the air fryer basket and cook for 5-7 minutes, shaking halfway through.
6. In a large pot, Combine cooked meatballs, vegetables, diced tomatoes, black beans, chicken broth, and spices.
7. Transfer pot to air fryer basket and cook for 15 minutes at 350°F (175°C), stirring halfway through.

Serving suggestion: Garnish with a sprinkle of fresh cilantro and a dollop of Greek yogurt if desired.

Nutritional Information (per serving): Calories: 350 | Protein: 30g| Carbohydrates: 25g | Fiber: 8g | Fat: 15g | Cholesterol: 70mg | Sodium: 450mg | Potassium: 800mg

Classic Minestrone Made Low-Carb

Prep. time: 15 min | **Cook time:** 25 min | **Servings:** 4

Ingredients:

- 1 medium zucchini, diced
- 1 medium yellow squash, diced
- 1 red bell pepper, diced
- 1 cup cauliflower florets
- 1 small onion, diced
- 2 cloves garlic, minced
- 1 can (14.5 oz) diced tomatoes, no salt added
- 4 cups low-sodium vegetable broth
- 1 can (15 oz) cannellini beans, drained and rinsed
- 2 cups chopped kale
- 1 tsp dried basil
- 1 tsp dried oregano
- 1/4 tsp red pepper flakes (optional)
- Salt and pepper to taste
- 2 tbsp olive oil
- 1 tbsp grated Parmesan cheese per serving (optional)

Directions:

1. Preheat the air fryer to 400°F (200°C).
2. In a large bowl, toss zucchini, yellow squash, bell pepper, cauliflower, onion, and garlic with 1 tbsp olive oil, basil, oregano, salt, and pepper.
3. Transfer the vegetable mixture to an air fryer basket. Cook for 10-12 minutes, shaking basket halfway through, until vegetables are lightly browned.
4. Combine roasted vegetables, diced tomatoes, broth, and cannellini beans in a large pot.
5. Place pot in air fryer basket and cook at 350°F (175°C) for 10 minutes.
6. Add kale and red pepper flakes. Continue cooking for 5 more minutes.
7. Taste and adjust seasoning if needed.

Serving suggestion: Ladle soup into bowls and drizzle with remaining olive oil. Sprinkle with Parmesan cheese if desired.

Nutritional Information (per serving): Calories: 250 | Protein: 12g | Carbohydrates: 30g | Fiber: 10g | Fat: 10g | Cholesterol: 0mg | Sodium: 400mg | Potassium: 700mg

Chicken Meatball Italian Wedding Soup

Prep. time: 20 min | **Cook time:** 25 min | **Servings:** 4

Ingredients:

- 1 lb ground chicken breast
- 1/4 cup almond flour
- 1 egg
- 2 cloves garlic, minced
- 1 tsp dried oregano
- 1 tsp dried basil
- 1/4 cup grated Parmesan cheese
- 4 cups low-sodium chicken broth
- 2 cups chopped escarole or spinach
- 1 medium carrot, diced
- 1 small onion, diced
- 1 celery stalk, diced
- 1 tbsp olive oil
- Salt and pepper to taste

Directions:

1. Preheat the air fryer to 375°F (190°C).
2. Mix ground chicken, almond flour, egg, half the garlic, half the herbs, Parmesan, salt, and pepper in a bowl. Form into 16 small meatballs.
3. Place meatballs in the air fryer basket. Cook for 10 minutes, shaking halfway through.
4. While meatballs cook, in a pot, sauté onion, carrot, celery, and remaining garlic in olive oil for 5 minutes.
5. Add broth to pot and bring to a simmer.
6. Transfer cooked meatballs to the pot.
7. Place pot in air fryer basket. Cook at 350°F (175°C) for 10 minutes.
8. Add escarole/spinach and remaining herbs. Cook for 5 more minutes.

Serving suggestion: Garnish with additional Parmesan if desired.

Nutritional Information (per serving): Calories: 280 | Protein: 30g | Carbohydrates: 8g | Fiber: 2g | Fat: 15g | Cholesterol: 110mg | Sodium: 450mg | Potassium: 600mg

Turkey

Turkey & Vegetable Stir Fry

Prep. time: 15 min **Cook time:** 20 min **Servings:** 4

Ingredients:

- 1 lb turkey breast, cut into bite-sized pieces
- 2 cups broccoli florets
- 1 red bell pepper, sliced
- 1 cup snap peas
- 1 small onion, sliced
- 2 cloves garlic, minced
- 1 tbsp grated ginger
- 2 tbsp low-sodium soy sauce
- 1 tbsp rice vinegar
- 1 tsp sesame oil
- 1 tbsp olive oil
- 1 tsp stevia (optional)
- Salt and pepper to taste

Directions:

1. Preheat the air fryer to 400°F (200°C).
2. In a bowl, mix turkey with 1 tbsp soy sauce, half the garlic, and half the ginger. Let marinate for 10 minutes.
3. Place the turkey in an air fryer basket. Cook for 8-10 minutes, shaking halfway through.
4. While the turkey cooks, mix the remaining soy sauce, rice vinegar, sesame oil, and stevia (if using) in a small bowl.
5. Remove the turkey from the basket. Add the vegetables, olive oil, remaining garlic, and ginger to the basket. Cook for 5-7 minutes, shaking halfway through.
6. Return the turkey to the basket with vegetables. Pour sauce over and toss to coat.
7. Cook for 2-3 minutes until everything is hot and well combined.

Serving suggestion: Serve over cauliflower rice or with a side of edamame for extra protein and fiber.

Nutritional Information (per serving): Calories: 250 | Protein: 30g | Carbohydrates: 10g | Fiber: 3g | Fat: 11g | Cholesterol: 65mg | Sodium: 400mg | Potassium: 550mg

Low-Carb Turkey Stuffed Bell Peppers

Prep. time: 15 min **Cook time:** 20 min **Servings:** 4

Ingredients:

- 4 medium bell peppers, halved and seeds removed
- 1 lb lean ground turkey
- 1 cup riced cauliflower
- 1/2 cup diced onion
- 2 cloves garlic, minced
- 1 can (14.5 oz) diced tomatoes, drained
- 1 tsp dried oregano
- 1 tsp ground cumin
- 1/2 tsp smoked paprika
- 1/4 cup grated Parmesan cheese
- Salt and pepper to taste
- 1 tbsp olive oil

Directions:

1. Preheat the air fryer to 375°F (190°C).
2. Mix turkey, cauliflower rice, onion, garlic, tomatoes, spices, and half the Parmesan in a bowl.
3. Brush bell pepper halves with olive oil and fill with turkey.
4. Place stuffed peppers in an air fryer basket, working in batches if necessary.
5. Cook for 15-18 minutes, until peppers are tender and filling is cooked through.
6. Sprinkle remaining Parmesan on top and cook for 2 minutes.

Serving suggestion: Serve with a side salad of mixed greens.

Nutritional Information (per serving - 2 pepper halves): Calories: 280 | Protein: 30g | Carbohydrates: 15g | Fiber: 5g | Fat: 13g | Cholesterol: 70mg | Sodium: 350mg | Potassium: 700mg

Zesty Lemon-Garlic Turkey Breast

Prep. time: 10 min **Cook time:** 30 min **Servings:** 4

Ingredients:

- 1 lb turkey breast, boneless and skinless
- 2 tbsp olive oil
- 2 tbsp lemon juice
- 2 cloves garlic, minced
- 1 tsp dried rosemary
- 1 tsp dried thyme
- 1/2 tsp salt
- 1/4 tsp black pepper
- Lemon zest from 1 lemon

Directions:

1. Preheat the air fryer to 375°F (190°C).
2. Mix olive oil, lemon juice, garlic, herbs, salt, pepper, and lemon zest in a bowl.
3. Coat turkey breast with the mixture.
4. Place the turkey in an air fryer basket.
5. Cook for 25-30 minutes, flipping halfway through, until internal temperature reaches 165°F (74°C).
6. Let rest for 5 minutes before slicing.

Serving suggestion: Serve with roasted non-starchy vegetables like broccoli or Brussels sprouts.

Nutritional Information (per serving): Calories: 220 | Protein: 28g | Carbohydrates: 1g | Fiber: 0g | Fat: 12g | Cholesterol: 70mg | Sodium: 340mg | Potassium: 350mg

Crispy Turkey Tacos with Avocado Crema

Prep. time: 15 min **Cook time:** 20 min **Servings:** 4

Ingredients:

- 1 lb ground turkey
- 12 small low-carb tortillas
- 1 cup shredded lettuce
- 1/2 cup diced tomatoes
- 1/4 cup diced red onion
- 2 tbsp olive oil
- 2 tsp chili powder
- 1 tsp ground cumin
- 1 tsp smoked paprika
- 1/2 tsp garlic powder
- Salt and pepper to taste

- 1 ripe avocado
- 1/4 cup Greek yogurt
- 2 tbsp lime juice
- 1 clove garlic
- Salt to taste

Directions:

1. Preheat the air fryer to 380°F (193°C).
2. Mix ground turkey with 1 tbsp olive oil and all spices.
3. Cook turkey in air fryer for 8-10 minutes, stirring halfway.
4. Remove turkey. Brush tortillas with remaining oil and air fry in batches for 2-3 minutes until crispy.
5. For crema, blend all ingredients until smooth.
6. Assemble tacos with turkey, lettuce, tomatoes, onion, and crema.

Serving suggestion: Add a side of sliced bell peppers or cucumber for extra crunch and nutrients.

Nutritional Information (per serving - 3 tacos): Calories: 420 | Protein: 30g | Carbohydrates: 25g | Fiber: 12g | Fat: 25g | Cholesterol: 60mg | Sodium: 400mg | Potassium: 600mg

Turkey Tenderloin with Roasted Vegetables

Prep. time: 15 min **Cook time:** 25 min **Servings:** 4

Ingredients:

- 1 lb turkey tenderloin
- 2 cups Brussels sprouts, halved
- 1 medium zucchini, sliced
- 1 red bell pepper, chopped
- 1 tbsp olive oil
- 1 tsp dried thyme
- 1 tsp dried rosemary
- 1 tsp garlic powder
- 1/2 tsp salt
- 1/4 tsp black pepper
- 1 lemon, juiced

Directions:

1. Preheat the air fryer to 375°F (190°C).
2. Mix herbs, garlic powder, salt, and pepper in a small bowl.
3. Rub turkey with half the herb mixture and 1 tsp olive oil.
4. Toss vegetables with remaining oil and herbs.
5. Place turkey in an air fryer basket, surrounded by vegetables.
6. Cook for 20-25 minutes, shaking basket halfway through.
7. Remove when the turkey reaches 165°F (74°C) internal temperature.
8. Let turkey rest for 5 minutes before slicing. Drizzle all with lemon juice.

Serving suggestion: Pair with a small side salad of mixed greens.

Nutritional Information (per serving): Calories: 250 | Protein: 30g | Carbohydrates: 10g | Fiber: 4g | Fat: 11g | Cholesterol: 65mg | Sodium: 350mg | Potassium: 700mg

Spicy Ground Turkey Lettuce Wraps

Prep. time: 10 min **Cook time:** 15 min **Servings:** 4

Ingredients:

- 1 lb lean ground turkey (93% lean)
- 1 tbsp olive oil
- 1/2 cup diced onion
- 2 cloves garlic, minced
- 1 tbsp grated ginger
- 1 red bell pepper, diced
- 1/4 cup water chestnuts, chopped
- 2 tbsp low-sodium soy sauce
- 1 tbsp rice vinegar
- 1 tsp sesame oil
- 1 tsp sriracha sauce (or to taste)
- 1 head butter lettuce, leaves separated
- 2 green onions, sliced (for garnish)

Directions:

1. Preheat the air fryer to 375°F (190°C).
2. Mix turkey, onion, garlic, ginger, bell pepper, and olive oil in a bowl.
3. Spread mixture in an air fryer basket.
4. Cook for 10 minutes, stirring halfway.
5. Add water chestnuts, soy sauce, vinegar, sesame oil, and sriracha.
6. Cook for 5 more minutes, stirring once.

Serving suggestion: For those who prefer heat, serve with extra sriracha or a low-sugar sweet chili sauce on the side.

Nutritional Information (per serving): Calories: 250 | Protein: 28g | Carbohydrates: 8g | Dietary Fiber: 2g | Net Carbs: 6g | Fat: 13g (of which saturated: 3g) | Cholesterol: 70mg | Sodium: 320mg | Potassium: 450mg

Rosemary & Garlic Infused Turkey Legs

Prep. time: 10 min **Cook time:** 45 min +2 hours marinating **Servings:** 4

Ingredients:

- 4 turkey legs (about 1 lb each)
- 2 tbsp olive oil
- 4 cloves garlic, minced
- 2 tbsp fresh rosemary, chopped
- 1 tsp lemon zest
- 1 tsp salt
- 1/2 tsp black pepper
- 1/4 tsp paprika

Directions:

1. Mix olive oil, garlic, rosemary, lemon zest, salt, pepper, and paprika in a bowl.
2. Rub mixture over turkey legs. Marinate in refrigerator for 2 hours.
3. Preheat the air fryer to 350°F (175°C).
4. Place turkey legs in an air fryer basket, skin side down.
5. Cook for 20 minutes. Flip legs.
6. Cook another 20-25 minutes until the internal temperature reaches 165°F (74°C).

Serving suggestion: Pair with roasted non-starchy vegetables like broccoli or Brussels sprouts.

Nutritional Information (per serving - 1 turkey leg): Calories: 380 | Protein: 48g | Carbohydrates: 1g | Dietary Fiber: 0.5g | Net Carbs: 0.5g | Fat: 20g (of which saturated: 5g) | Cholesterol: 165mg | Sodium: 650mg | Potassium: 520mg

Turkey Meatball Soup with Spiralized Veggies

Prep. time: 20 min **Cook time:** 25 min **Servings:** 4

Ingredients:

For meatballs:
- 1 lb lean ground turkey (93% lean)
- 1/4 cup almond flour
- 1 egg
- 1 tsp garlic powder
- 1 tsp dried oregano
- 1/2 tsp salt
- 1/4 tsp black pepper

For soup:
- 6 cups low-sodium chicken broth
- 2 medium zucchinis, spiralized
- 2 medium carrots, spiralized
- 1 cup diced celery
- 1 cup diced onion
- 2 cloves garlic, minced
- 1 tbsp olive oil
- 1 tsp dried thyme
- 1 bay leaf
- Salt and pepper to taste

Directions:

1. Mix meatball ingredients and form 20 small meatballs.
2. Preheat the air fryer to 375°F (190°C).
3. Air fry meatballs for 10-12 minutes; shake halfway.
4. Sauté onion, celery, and garlic in a pot with oil.
5. Add broth, carrots, thyme, bay leaf. Simmer for 10 minutes.
6. Add zucchini and meatballs. Cook for 5 minutes.
7. Season, serve hot.

Serving suggestion: Garnish with fresh parsley.

Nutritional Information (per serving): Calories: 290 | Protein: 30g | Carbohydrates: 15g | Fiber: 4g | Net Carbs: 11g | Fat: 14g (saturated: 3g) | Cholesterol: 105mg | Sodium: 620mg | Potassium: 780mg

Balsamic Glazed Brussels Sprouts & Ground Turkey

Prep. time: 15 min | **Cook time:** 20 min | **Servings:** 4

Ingredients:

- 1 lb lean ground turkey (93% lean)
- 1 lb Brussels sprouts, halved
- 2 tbsp olive oil
- 2 tbsp balsamic vinegar
- 1 tsp garlic powder
- 1 tsp dried thyme
- 1/2 tsp salt
- 1/4 tsp black pepper
- 1 tbsp Dijon mustard
- 1 tsp erythritol (optional for sweetness)

Directions:

1. Mix ground turkey with half of garlic powder, thyme, salt, and pepper.
2. Preheat the air fryer to 375°F (190°C).
3. Air fry turkey for 8-10 minutes, stirring halfway.
4. Remove the turkey and set aside.
5. Toss Brussels sprouts with 1 tbsp olive oil and remaining spices.
6. Air fry sprouts for 10 minutes, shaking basket halfway.
7. Mix balsamic vinegar, Dijon, remaining oil, and erythritol.
8. Add turkey to sprouts and drizzle with balsamic mixture.
9. Air fry for 2-3 minutes more.

Serving suggestion: Serve hot, garnished with fresh thyme if desired.

Nutritional Information (per serving): Calories: 310 | Protein: 29g | Carbohydrates: 12g | Fiber: 4g | Net Carbs: 8g | Fat: 18g (saturated: 4g) | Cholesterol: 85mg | Sodium: 450mg | Potassium: 700mg

Stuffed Portobello Mushrooms with Ground Turkey & Feta Cheese

Prep. time: 15 min | **Cook time:** 20 min | **Servings:** 4

Ingredients:

- 4 large portobello mushrooms
- 1 lb lean ground turkey (93% lean)
- 1/2 cup crumbled feta cheese
- 1 cup fresh spinach, chopped
- 1/4 cup diced red bell pepper
- 2 cloves garlic, minced
- 1 tbsp olive oil
- 1 tsp dried oregano
- 1/2 tsp dried thyme
- 1/4 tsp salt
- 1/4 tsp black pepper

Directions:

1. Remove stems from mushrooms and chop finely.
2. Preheat the air fryer to 375°F (190°C).
3. Sauté turkey, chopped stems, garlic, and bell pepper in a pan until the turkey is cooked.
4. Add spinach, oregano, thyme, salt, and pepper. Cook until spinach wilts.
5. Remove from heat, stir in half the feta cheese.
6. Brush mushroom caps with olive oil.
7. Stuff mushrooms with turkey mixture and top with remaining feta.
8. Air fry for 10-12 minutes until mushrooms are tender and cheese is slightly golden.

Serving suggestion: Serve hot, garnished with fresh herbs if desired. Pair with a small side salad for added fiber and nutrients.

Nutritional Information (per serving - 1 stuffed mushroom): Calories: 280 | Protein: 28g | Carbohydrates: 7g | Fiber: 2g | Net Carbs: 5g | Fat: 17g (saturated: 6g) | Cholesterol: 85mg | Sodium: 450mg | Potassium: 650mg

Thanksgiving-Style Sliced Turkey Breast

Prep. time: 10 min   **Cook time:** 27 min   **Servings:** 4

Ingredients:

- 1.5 lbs turkey breast, boneless and skinless
- 1 tbsp olive oil
- 1 tsp dried thyme
- 1 tsp dried rosemary
- 1 tsp dried sage
- 1/2 tsp garlic powder
- 1/2 tsp onion powder
- 1/2 tsp salt
- 1/4 tsp black pepper
- 1 tbsp sugar-free maple syrup

Directions:

1. Mix olive oil, herbs, spices, and sugar-free maple syrup in a bowl.
2. Rub mixture all over turkey breast.
3. Preheat the air fryer to 350°F (175°C).
4. Place the turkey in an air fryer basket.
5. Cook for 25-30 minutes, flipping halfway through.
6. Check internal temperature reaches 165°F (74°C).
7. Let rest for 5 minutes before slicing.

Serving suggestion: Slice and serve with a side of roasted non-starchy vegetables like Brussels sprouts or green beans.

Nutritional Information (per serving): Calories: 220 | Protein: 38g | Carbohydrates: 1g | Fiber: 0g | Net Carbs: 1g | Fat: 7g (saturated: 1.5g) | Cholesterol: 95mg | Sodium: 360mg | Potassium: 450mg

Turkey Zucchini Boats with Mozzarella Topping

Prep. time: 15 min   **Cook time:** 20 min   **Servings:** 4

Ingredients:

- 4 medium zucchinis
- 1 lb lean ground turkey (93% lean)
- 1/2 cup diced onion
- 2 cloves garlic, minced
- 1 cup crushed tomatoes, no sugar added
- 1 tsp dried basil
- 1 tsp dried oregano
- 1/4 tsp red pepper flakes (optional)
- 1/2 tsp salt
- 1/4 tsp black pepper
- 1/2 cup shredded part-skim mozzarella cheese
- 2 tbsp grated Parmesan cheese

Directions:

1. Cut zucchini in half lengthwise, scoop out centers.
2. Cook turkey, onion, and garlic in a pan until turkey is browned.
3. Add tomatoes, herbs, spices. Simmer for 5 minutes.
4. Preheat the air fryer to 375°F (190°C).
5. Fill zucchini boats with turkey mixture.
6. Air fry for 10 minutes.
7. Top with cheeses, air fry for 5 more minutes.

Serving suggestion: Serve hot, garnished with fresh basil if desired.

Nutritional Information (per serving - 2 zucchini boats): Calories: 290 | Protein: 32g | Carbohydrates: 14g | Fiber: 4g | Net Carbs: 10g | Fat: 13g (saturated: 5g) | Cholesterol: 80mg | Sodium: 520mg | Potassium: 950mg

BBQ Basted Mini-Turkey Meatloaves

Prep. time: 15 min **Cook time:** 20 min **Servings:** 4 (2 mini-loaves each)

Ingredients:

- 1 lb ground turkey
- 1/2 cup almond flour
- 1 egg
- 1/4 cup finely chopped onion
- 2 cloves garlic, minced
- 1 tsp dried oregano
- 1 tsp smoked paprika
- 1/4 tsp black pepper and 1/2 tsp salt

- 1/4 cup tomato paste
- 2 tbsp apple cider vinegar
- 1 tbsp Worcestershire sauce
- 1 tsp liquid smoke
- 2 tbsp erythritol or preferred sugar substitute
- 1/2 tsp garlic powder
- 1/2 tsp onion powder

Directions:

1. Preheat the air fryer to 375°F (190°C).
2. Mix ground turkey, almond flour, egg, onion, garlic, and spices in a bowl.
3. Form the mixture into 8 small loaves.
4. Place loaves in an air fryer basket, leaving space between each.
5. Cook for 10 minutes.
6. Meanwhile, mix all BBQ sauce ingredients in a small bowl.
7. After 10 minutes, brush loaves with BBQ sauce.
8. Cook for another 5-7 minutes until internal temperature reaches 165°F (74°C).

Serving suggestion: Serve with a side of roasted low-carb vegetables like broccoli or cauliflower.

Nutritional Information (per serving - 2 mini-loaves): Calories: 280 | Protein: 28g | Carbohydrates: 8g | Fiber: 3g | Fat: 16g | Cholesterol: 120mg | Sodium: 450mg | Potassium: 400mg

Asian-Inspired Ground Turkey Wraps

Prep. time: 15 min **Cook time:** 10 min **Servings:** 4

Ingredients:

- 1 lb lean ground turkey (93% lean)
- 1 tbsp sesame oil
- 2 cloves garlic, minced
- 1 tbsp grated fresh ginger
- 1/4 cup low-sodium soy sauce
- 1 tbsp rice vinegar
- 1 tsp monk fruit sweetener
- 1 cup shredded carrots
- 1 cup sliced bell peppers
- 4 large lettuce leaves (romaine or butter lettuce)
- 1 tbsp sesame seeds
- 2 green onions, sliced

Directions:

1. Preheat the air fryer to 375°F (190°C).
2. Mix soy sauce, vinegar, sweetener, and half the sesame oil.
3. Cook turkey, garlic, and ginger in the air fryer for 5 minutes.
4. Add carrots and peppers, cook 3 more minutes.
5. Stir in the sauce mixture and cook for 2 more minutes.
6. Sprinkle with sesame seeds and green onions.
7. Serve in lettuce wraps.

Serving suggestion: Serve the turkey mixture in lettuce wraps garnished with extra sesame seeds and green onions.

Nutritional Information (per serving - 1 wrap): Calories: 250 | Protein: 28g | Carbohydrates: 8g | Fiber: 2g | Net Carbs: 6g | Fat: 13g (saturated: 3g) | Cholesterol: 70mg | Sodium: 550mg | Potassium: 450mg

Hearty Turkey Sausage Casserole

Prep. time: 15 min | Cook time: 25 min | Servings: 4

Ingredients:

- 1 lb turkey sausage, casings removed
- 2 cups cauliflower rice
- 1 medium zucchini, diced
- 1 red bell pepper, diced
- 1 cup mushrooms, sliced
- 1/2 cup onion, diced
- 2 cloves garlic, minced
- 1 tsp dried oregano
- 1 tsp dried basil
- 1/4 tsp red pepper flakes (optional)
- 1/2 cup low-fat mozzarella cheese, shredded
- 2 tbsp olive oil
- Salt and pepper to taste

Directions:

1. Preheat the air fryer to 375°F (190°C).
2. Cook turkey sausage in a pan, breaking it up.
3. Mix all ingredients except cheese in a large bowl.
4. Transfer to an air fryer-safe dish.
5. Cook for 15 minutes, stirring halfway.
6. Add cheese on top and cook for 5 more minutes.
7. Let rest for 5 minutes before serving.

Serving suggestion: Serve hot, garnished with fresh basil if desired. Pair with a small side salad for extra fiber and nutrients.

Nutritional Information (per serving): Calories: 320 | Protein: 28g | Carbohydrates: 10g | Fiber: 3g | Net Carbs: 7g | Fat: 20g (saturated: 5g) | Cholesterol: 70mg | Sodium: 580mg | Potassium: 620mg

Parmesan-Crusted Turkey Tenders

Prep. time: 15 min | Cook time: 12 min | Servings: 4

Ingredients:

- 1 lb turkey breast tenderloins
- 1/2 cup grated Parmesan cheese
- 1/4 cup almond flour
- 1 tsp dried oregano
- 1 tsp garlic powder
- 1/2 tsp paprika
- 1/4 tsp black pepper
- 1/4 tsp salt
- 1 large egg
- 1 tbsp Dijon mustard
- 1 tbsp olive oil

Directions:

1. Mix Parmesan, almond flour, oregano, garlic powder, paprika, pepper, and salt in a shallow dish.
2. Whisk egg, Dijon mustard, and olive oil in another dish.
3. Dip each turkey tender in egg mixture, then coat with Parmesan mixture.
4. Place tenders in the air fryer basket, not overcrowding.
5. Air fry at 380°F (193°C) for 6 minutes.
6. Flip tenders and cook for another 5-6 minutes until golden and crispy.
7. Ensure internal temperature reaches 165°F (74°C).

Serving suggestion: Pair with a mixed green salad or air-fried vegetables for a complete meal.

Nutrition per serving: Calories: 290 | Protein: 38g | Carbohydrates: 3g | Fiber: 1g | Fat: 15g | Cholesterol: 120mg | Sodium: 480mg | Potassium: 400mg

Sesame-Ginger Turkey Meatballs

Prep. time: 15 min **Cook time:** 12 min **Servings:** 4

Ingredients:

- 1 lb ground turkey (93% lean)
- 1/4 cup almond flour
- 1 large egg
- 2 tbsp grated fresh ginger
- 2 cloves garlic, minced
- 2 tbsp coconut aminos
- 1 tbsp sesame oil
- 2 tbsp chopped green onions
- 1 tbsp sesame seeds
- 1/4 tsp black pepper
- 1/4 tsp salt

Directions:

1. Mix all ingredients in a large bowl until well combined.
2. Form mixture into 16 meatballs (about 1.5 inches each).
3. Place meatballs in an air fryer basket, leaving space between each.
4. Air fry at 375°F (190°C) for 12 minutes, shaking basket halfway through.
5. Ensure internal temperature reaches 165°F (74°C).

Serving suggestion: Serve over cauliflower rice or zucchini noodles with steamed broccoli.

Nutrition per serving: Calories: 280 | Protein: 32g | Carbohydrates: 5g | Fiber: 2g | Fat: 16g | Cholesterol: 130mg | Sodium: 380mg | Potassium: 400mg

Buffalo-Style Turkey Drumsticks

Prep. time: 10 min **Cook time:** 25 min **Servings:** 4

Ingredients:

- 4 turkey drumsticks, skin removed
- 2 tbsp olive oil
- 1 tsp garlic powder
- 1 tsp paprika
- 1/2 tsp salt
- 1/4 tsp black pepper

Buffalo Sauce:

- 1/4 cup hot sauce
- 2 tbsp butter
- 1 tsp apple cider vinegar
- 1/4 tsp garlic powder

Directions:

1. Mix olive oil, garlic powder, paprika, salt, and pepper in a bowl.
2. Rub mixture over turkey drumsticks.
3. Place drumsticks in the air fryer basket without overcrowding.
4. Air fry at 380°F (193°C) for 20-25 minutes, turning halfway through.
5. Meanwhile, prepare buffalo sauce: melt butter and mix with hot sauce, vinegar, and garlic powder.
6. Brush drumsticks with buffalo sauce in the last 2 minutes of cooking.
7. Ensure internal temperature reaches 165°F (74°C).

Serving suggestion: Serve with celery sticks and a low-fat blue cheese dip.

Nutrition per serving: Calories: 310 | Protein: 35g | Carbohydrates: 1g | Fiber: 0g | Fat: 19g | Cholesterol: 130mg | Sodium: 620mg | Potassium: 380mg

Greek-Style Turkey Burgers with Tzatziki

Prep. time: 15 min **Cook time:** 12 min **Servings:** 4

Ingredients:

- 1 lb ground turkey (93% lean)
- 1/4 cup crumbled feta cheese
- 1/4 cup finely chopped red onion
- 2 tbsp chopped fresh parsley
- 1 tsp dried oregano
- 1 clove garlic, minced
- 1/2 tsp salt
- 1/4 tsp black pepper

- 1/2 cup Greek yogurt (0% fat)
- 1/4 cup grated cucumber, squeezed dry
- 1 tsp lemon juice
- 1/4 tsp dried dill
- 1 small garlic clove, minced
- Salt and pepper to taste

Directions:

1. Mix all burger ingredients in a bowl. Form into 4 patties.
2. Preheat the air fryer to 375°F (190°C).
3. Place patties in the air fryer basket, not overcrowding.
4. Cook for 12 minutes, flipping halfway through.
5. Ensure internal temperature reaches 165°F (74°C).
6. While burgers cook, mix tzatziki ingredients in a small bowl.

Serving suggestion: Serve burgers on lettuce wraps with tzatziki, sliced tomatoes, and red onions.

Nutrition per serving (1 burger with tzatziki): Calories: 260 | Protein: 32g | Carbohydrates: 5g | Fiber: 1g | Fat: 13g | Cholesterol: 90mg | Sodium: 550mg | Potassium: 400mg

Teriyaki Turkey Skewers with Pineapple

Prep. time: 10 min + 20 min marinating **Cook time:** 15 min **Servings:** 4

Ingredients:

- 1 lb turkey breast, cut into 1-inch cubes
- 1 cup fresh pineapple chunks
- 1 medium bell pepper, cut into 1-inch pieces

Teriyaki Marinade:

- 3 tbsp coconut aminos
- 1 tbsp rice vinegar
- 1 tbsp sesame oil
- 1 tsp grated fresh ginger
- 1 clove garlic, minced
- 1 tbsp erythritol or stevia blend

Directions:

1. Mix marinade ingredients in a bowl.
2. Add turkey cubes to marinade and refrigerate for 30 minutes.
3. Thread turkey, pineapple, and bell pepper onto 8 skewers.
4. Preheat the air fryer to 375°F (190°C).
5. Place skewers in the air fryer basket, not overcrowding.
6. Cook for 10-12 minutes, turning halfway through.
7. Ensure turkey reaches 165°F (74°C) internal temperature.

Serving suggestion: Serve over cauliflower rice with steamed broccoli.

Nutrition per serving (2 skewers): Calories: 220 | Protein: 28g | Carbohydrates: 10g | Fiber: 1g | Fat: 8g | Cholesterol: 65mg | Sodium: 280mg | Potassium: 450mg

Chicken

Chicken Breast with Steamed Broccoli

Prep. time: 10 min **Cook time:** 20 min **Servings:** 4

Ingredients:

- 4 (6 oz each) boneless, skinless chicken breasts
- 2 tbsp olive oil
- 2 tbsp lemon juice
- 1 tsp lemon zest
- 2 cloves garlic, minced
- 1 tsp dried oregano
- 1/2 tsp salt
- 1/4 tsp black pepper
- 4 cups broccoli florets

Directions:

1. Preheat the air fryer to 375°F (190°C).
2. Mix olive oil, lemon juice, zest, garlic, oregano, salt, and pepper in a bowl.
3. Coat chicken breasts with the mixture.
4. Place chicken in an air fryer basket.
5. Cook for 10 minutes, flip, then cook 8-10 more minutes until internal temperature reaches 165°F (74°C).
6. While the chicken cooks, steam broccoli in a separate steamer or microwave.
7. Let chicken rest for 3-5 minutes before serving.

Serving suggestion: Serve chicken over steamed broccoli, drizzling any remaining cooking juices over the top.

Nutritional Information (per serving): Calories: 280 | Protein: 35g | Carbohydrates: 8g | Fiber: 3g | Fat: 12g | Cholesterol: 95mg | Sodium: 380mg | Potassium: 700mg

Savory Garlic & Herb Chicken Drumsticks

Prep. time: 10 min **Cook time:** 25 min **Servings:** 4

Ingredients:

- 8 chicken drumsticks, skin removed
- 2 tbsp olive oil
- 3 cloves garlic, minced
- 1 tsp dried thyme
- 1 tsp dried rosemary
- 1 tsp dried parsley
- 1/2 tsp paprika
- 1/2 tsp salt
- 1/4 tsp black pepper
- Lemon wedges for serving

Directions:

1. Preheat the air fryer to 380°F (193°C).
2. Mix olive oil, garlic, herbs, and spices in a bowl.
3. Coat drumsticks evenly with the mixture.
4. Arrange drumsticks in the air fryer basket, not overcrowding.
5. Cook for 10 minutes, then flip.
6. Cook for another 10-15 minutes until internal temperature reaches 165°F (74°C).
7. Let rest for 3-5 minutes before serving.

Serving suggestion: Serve with mixed greens or roasted non-starchy vegetables. Squeeze fresh lemon over the chicken for added flavor.

Nutritional Information (per serving - 2 drumsticks): Calories: 250 | Protein: 28g | Carbohydrates: 1g | Fiber: 0g | Fat: 15g | Cholesterol: 130mg | Sodium: 360mg | Potassium: 300mg

Healthy Chicken Cordon Bleu

Prep. time: 15 min   **Cook time:** 20 min   **Servings:** 4

Ingredients:

- 4 (6 oz each) boneless, skinless chicken breasts
- 4 slices lean ham (2 oz total)
- 4 slices Swiss cheese (2 oz total)
- 1/2 cup almond flour
- 1 egg, beaten
- 1 tsp garlic powder
- 1 tsp dried thyme
- 1/2 tsp salt
- 1/4 tsp black pepper
- Cooking spray (olive oil based)

Directions:

1. Preheat the air fryer to 375°F (190°C).
2. Butterfly each chicken breast and place ham and cheese inside. Close and secure with toothpicks.
3. Mix almond flour, garlic powder, thyme, salt, and pepper in a shallow dish.
4. Dip each stuffed breast in egg, then coat with almond flour.
5. Lightly spray the air fryer basket with cooking spray.
6. Place chicken in a basket, spray tops lightly with cooking spray.
7. Cook for 10 minutes, flip, spray again, and cook for 8-10 more minutes until internal temperature reaches 165°F (74°C).
8. Let rest for 3-5 minutes before serving.

Serving suggestion: Pair with steamed green beans or a side salad.

Nutritional Information (per serving): Calories: 340 | Protein: 45g | Carbohydrates: 5g | Fiber: 2g | Fat: 16g | Cholesterol: 145mg | Sodium: 580mg | Potassium: 500mg

Buffalo Chicken Wings with Celery Sticks

Prep. time: 10 min   **Cook time:** 25 min   **Servings:** 4

Ingredients:

- 2 lbs chicken wings, split into flats and drumettes
- 1 tbsp baking powder (aluminium-free)
- 1/2 tsp salt
- 1/4 tsp black pepper
- 1/4 cup hot sauce (like Frank's Red Hot)
- 2 tbsp butter, melted
- 1 tsp apple cider vinegar
- 1/4 tsp garlic powder
- 4 celery stalks, cut into sticks

Directions:

1. Preheat the air fryer to 380°F (193°C).
2. Pat wings dry with paper towels.
3. Toss wings with baking powder, salt, and pepper in a large bowl.
4. Arrange wings in an air fryer basket in a single layer.
5. Cook for 10 minutes, shake the basket, and cook 10-15 more minutes until crispy and the temperature reaches 165°F (74°C).
6. Mix hot sauce, melted butter, vinegar, and garlic powder while cooking wings.
7. Toss cooked wings in a sauce mixture.

Serving suggestion: Serve immediately with celery sticks on the side.

Nutritional Information (per serving): Calories: 380 | Protein: 28g | Carbohydrates: 2g | Fiber: 1g | Fat: 29g | Cholesterol: 145mg | Sodium: 720mg | Potassium: 250mg

Crispy Sesame Ginger Chicken Thighs

Prep. time: 15 min + 30 marinating | *Cook time:* 25 min | *Servings:* 4

Ingredients:

- 8 boneless, skinless chicken thighs (about 2 lbs)
- 2 tbsp low-sodium soy sauce
- 1 tbsp sesame oil
- 1 tbsp rice vinegar
- 1 tbsp grated fresh ginger
- 2 cloves garlic, minced
- 1 tbsp sesame seeds
- 1 tsp erythritol or preferred sugar substitute
- 1/4 tsp black pepper

Directions:

1. Mix soy sauce, sesame oil, vinegar, ginger, garlic, erythritol, and pepper in a bowl.
2. Marinate chicken in mixture for 30 minutes in the refrigerator.
3. Preheat air fryer to 380°F (193°C).
4. Remove chicken from marinade, shaking off excess. Sprinkle with sesame seeds.
5. Place chicken in an air fryer basket in a single layer.
6. Cook for 10 minutes, flip, then cook 10-15 more minutes until crispy and internal temperature reaches 165°F (74°C).

Serving suggestion: Serve with steamed broccoli or a mixed green salad.

Nutritional Information (per serving - 2 thighs): Calories: 300 | Protein: 35g | Carbohydrates: 2g | Fiber: 0g | Fat: 18g | Cholesterol: 170mg | Sodium: 380mg | Potassium: 400mg

Mediterranean Greek Salad with Grilled Chicken

Prep. time: 15 min | *Cook time:* 15 min | *Servings:* 4

Ingredients:

- 1 lb boneless, skinless chicken breast
- 4 cups mixed salad greens
- 1 cucumber, diced
- 1 cup cherry tomatoes, halved
- 1/2 red onion, thinly sliced
- 1/2 cup kalamata olives, pitted
- 1/2 cup crumbled feta cheese
- 2 tbsp olive oil
- 1 tbsp lemon juice
- 1 tsp dried oregano
- 1/2 tsp garlic powder
- Salt and pepper to taste

Directions:

1. Preheat the air fryer to 380°F (193°C).
2. Mix 1 tbsp olive oil, oregano, garlic powder, salt, 1 tsp lemon juice, and pepper.
3. Coat chicken with mixture and place in air fryer basket.
4. Cook chicken for 12-15 minutes, flipping halfway, until temperature reaches 165°F (74°C).
5. While chicken cooks, prepare salad by combining greens, cucumber, tomatoes, onion, olives, and feta in a large bowl.
6. Mix remaining olive oil and lemon juice for dressing.
7. Slice cooked chicken and add to salad.
8. Drizzle with dressing and toss gently.

Serving suggestion: Serve immediately, garnished with additional oregano if desired.

Nutritional Information (per serving): Calories: 320 | Protein: 30g | Carbohydrates: 8g | Fiber: 2g | Fat: 20g | Cholesterol: 85mg | Sodium: 550mg | Potassium: 600mg

Rosemary Garlic Roasted Whole Chicken

🍲 **Prep. time:** 15 min   🕐 **Cook time:** 55 min   🍴 **Servings:** 4

Ingredients:

- 1 whole chicken (3-4 lbs), giblets removed
- 2 tbsp olive oil
- 2 tbsp fresh rosemary, chopped
- 4 cloves garlic, minced
- 1 tsp salt
- 1/2 tsp black pepper
- 1 lemon, quartered

Directions:

1. Line the chicken dry with paper towels. Mix olive oil, rosemary, garlic, salt, and pepper in a small bowl.
2. Rub the mixture all over the chicken, including under the skin. Place lemon quarters in the cavity.
3. Preheat the air fryer to 360°F (180°C).
4. Place chicken breast-side down in the air fryer basket. Cook for 30 minutes.
5. Flip the chicken breast-side up. Cook for 20-30 minutes until the internal temperature reaches 165°F (74°C) at the thickest part.
6. Let rest 10 minutes before carving.

Serving suggestion: Pair with a side of roasted non-starchy vegetables.

Nutrition per serving (1/4 chicken): Calories: 330 | Protein: 38g | Carbohydrates: 2g | Fiber: 0.5g | Fat: 20g (6g saturated) | Cholesterol: 115mg | Sodium: 400mg | Potassium: 350mg

Teriyaki Glazed Drumsticks

🍲 **Prep. time:** 10 min + 30 marinating   🕐 **Cook time:** 25 min   🍴 **Servings:** 4

Ingredients:

- 8 chicken drumsticks, skin removed
- 1/4 cup low-sodium soy sauce
- 2 tbsp rice vinegar
- 1 tbsp sesame oil
- 2 cloves garlic, minced
- 1 tbsp fresh ginger, grated
- 2 tbsp erythritol or monk fruit sweetener
- 1 tsp xanthan gum
- 1 tbsp sesame seeds
- 2 green onions, chopped

Directions:

1. Mix a bowl of soy sauce, vinegar, sesame oil, garlic, ginger, and sweetener.
2. Place drumsticks in a zip-top bag and add half the marinade. Refrigerate for 30 minutes.
3. Preheat air fryer to 380°F (193°C).
4. Arrange drumsticks in the air fryer basket, not overcrowding.
5. Cook for 10 minutes, then flip and cook for another 8-10 minutes until internal temperature reaches 165°F (74°C).
6. Meanwhile, heat the remaining marinade in a small pan. Add xanthan gum and simmer until thickened.
7. Brush drumsticks with glaze and air fry for 2 more minutes.
8. Sprinkle with sesame seeds and green onions before serving.

Serving suggestion: Pair with cauliflower rice or a mixed green salad.

Nutrition per serving (2 drumsticks): Calories: 220 | Protein: 28g | Carbohydrates: 3g | Fiber: 1g | Fat: 11g (2.5g saturated) | Cholesterol: 130mg | Sodium: 480mg | Potassium: 300mg

Mexican Fiesta Stuffed Organic Chicken

Prep. time: 20 min | **Cook time:** 18 min | **Servings:** 4

Ingredients:

- 4 organic boneless, skinless chicken breasts (6 oz each)
- 1/2 cup diced bell peppers (mix of red, green, yellow)
- 1/4 cup diced onion
- 1/2 cup shredded cheddar cheese
- 1 jalapeno, seeded and minced (optional)
- 1 tsp ground cumin
- 1 tsp chili powder
- 1/2 tsp garlic powder
- 1/2 tsp smoked paprika
- Salt and pepper to taste
- 1 tbsp olive oil
- 1/4 cup chopped fresh cilantro

Directions:

1. Mix bell peppers, onion, cheese, jalapeno (if using), cumin, chili powder, garlic powder, and smoked paprika.
2. Cut a pocket in each chicken breast. Season inside and out with salt and pepper.
3. Stuff each breast with the vegetable-cheese mixture.
4. Brush chicken with olive oil and sprinkle with any remaining spices.
5. Preheat the air fryer to 375°F (190°C).
6. Place stuffed chicken breasts in the air fryer basket without overcrowding.
7. Cook for 15-18 minutes, flipping halfway through, until internal temperature reaches 165°F (74°C).
8. Let rest for 5 minutes before serving. Garnish with fresh cilantro.

Serving suggestion: Pair with a side of guacamole and sliced cherry tomatoes.

Nutrition per serving (1 stuffed chicken breast): Calories: 300 | Protein: 36g | Carbohydrates: 4g | Fiber: 1g | Fat: 16g (6g saturated) | Cholesterol: 110mg | Sodium: 320mg | Potassium: 500mg

Coconut Curry Crusted Chicken Tenders

Prep. time: 15 min | **Cook time:** 15 min | **Servings:** 4

Ingredients:

- 1 lb chicken tenders (about 8-10 pieces)
- 1 cup unsweetened shredded coconut
- 2 tbsp almond flour
- 1 tbsp curry powder
- 1 tsp turmeric
- 1/2 tsp garlic powder
- 1/2 tsp salt
- 1/4 tsp black pepper
- 1 large egg
- 1 tbsp water
- Olive oil spray

Directions:

1. In a shallow bowl, mix coconut, almond flour, curry powder, turmeric, garlic powder, salt, and pepper.
2. In another bowl, whisk an egg with water.
3. Dip each chicken tender in egg mixture, then coat with coconut.
4. Preheat the air fryer to 375°F (190°C).
5. Arrange coated tenders in air fryer basket, not overcrowding. Spray lightly with olive oil.
6. Cook for 6-7 minutes, flip, spray again, and cook for another 6-8 minutes until golden and temperature reaches 165°F (74°C).
7. Work in batches if necessary.

Serving suggestion: Serve with a side of cucumber raita (mix Greek yogurt, grated cucumber, mint, and a pinch of salt) and steamed broccoli.

Nutrition per serving (2-3 tenders): Calories: 290 | Protein: 25g | Carbohydrates: 8g | Fiber: 4g | Fat: 18g (12g saturated) | Cholesterol: 95mg | Sodium: 380mg | Potassium: 300mg

Parmesan Crusted Organic Chicken Fillets

Prep. time: 10 min | **Cook time:** 15 min | **Servings:** 4

Ingredients:

- 4 organic chicken breast fillets (4-5 oz each)
- 1 cup grated Parmesan cheese
- 1/4 cup almond flour
- 1 tsp dried oregano
- 1 tsp dried basil
- 1/2 tsp garlic powder
- 1/4 tsp black pepper
- 1 large egg
- 1 tbsp water
- Olive oil spray

Directions:

1. Mix Parmesan, almond flour, oregano, basil, garlic powder, and pepper in a shallow bowl.
2. In another bowl, whisk an egg with water.
3. Dip each chicken fillet in egg mixture, then coat with Parmesan mixture.
4. Preheat air fryer to 380°F (193°C).
5. Place coated fillets in an air fryer basket without overcrowding. Spray lightly with olive oil.
6. Cook for 6-7 minutes, flip, spray again, and cook for another 6-8 minutes until golden and temperature reaches 165°F (74°C).
7. Let rest for 3 minutes before serving.

Serving suggestion: Pair with roasted asparagus or a mixed green salad with vinaigrette dressing.

Nutrition per serving (1 chicken fillet): Calories: 290 | Protein: 35g | Carbohydrates: 2g | Fiber: 1g | Fat: 16g (7g saturated) | Cholesterol: 130mg | Sodium: 450mg | Potassium: 400mg

Caprese Style Stuffed Grilled-Chicken

Prep. time: 15 min | **Cook time:** 17 min | **Servings:** 4

Ingredients:

- 4 boneless, skinless chicken breasts (6 oz each)
- 4 oz fresh mozzarella, sliced
- 1 medium tomato, sliced
- 8 fresh basil leaves
- 2 tbsp olive oil
- 2 tbsp balsamic vinegar
- 1 tsp Dijon mustard
- 1 clove garlic, minced
- 1 tsp Italian seasoning
- Salt and pepper to taste

Directions:

1. Cut a pocket in each chicken breast.
2. Stuff each breast with mozzarella, tomato, and basil leaves.
3. Mix olive oil, 1 tbsp balsamic vinegar, mustard, garlic, Italian seasoning, salt, and pepper.
4. Brush mixture over chicken breasts.
5. Preheat the air fryer to 375°F (190°C).
6. Place stuffed chicken in an air fryer basket without overcrowding.
7. Cook for 15-18 minutes, flipping halfway, until internal temperature reaches 165°F (74°C).
8. Meanwhile, simmer the remaining 1 tbsp balsamic vinegar until slightly reduced for the glaze.
9. Let chicken rest for 5 minutes, then drizzle with balsamic glaze before serving.

Serving suggestion: Pair with a side of air-fried zucchini or a mixed green salad.

Nutrition per serving (1 stuffed chicken breast): Calories: 310 | Protein: 38g | Carbohydrates: 3g | Fiber: 0.5g | Fat: 17g (5g saturated) | Cholesterol: 110mg | Sodium: 300mg | Potassium: 450mg

BBQ Pulled Grilled-Chicken Lettuce Wraps

Prep. time: 15 min | **Cook time:** 25 min | **Servings:** 4

Ingredients:

- 1 lb boneless, skinless chicken breasts
- 1 tbsp olive oil
- 1 tbsp smoked paprika
- 1 tsp garlic powder
- 1 tsp onion powder
- 1 tsp cumin
- 1/2 tsp chili powder
- 1/4 tsp black pepper
- 1/4 cup sugar-free BBQ sauce
- 8 large lettuce leaves (Boston or Romaine)
- 1/4 cup red onion, finely chopped
- 1/4 cup fresh cilantro, chopped
- 1 lime, cut into wedges

Directions:

1. Mix paprika, garlic powder, onion powder, cumin, chili powder, and pepper in a bowl.
2. Rub chicken with olive oil, then coat with spice mixture.
3. Preheat air fryer to 380°F (193°C).
4. Place chicken in an air fryer basket and cook for 10-12 minutes.
5. Flip chicken and cook for another 8-10 minutes until internal temperature reaches 165°F (74°C).
6. Let chicken rest for 5 minutes, then shred using two forks.
7. Toss shredded chicken with sugar-free BBQ sauce.
8. Topped with red onion and cilantro, serve chicken in lettuce leaves. Serve with lime wedges.

Serving suggestion: Pair with a side of cucumber and jicama sticks.

Nutrition per serving (2 lettuce wraps): Calories: 220 | Protein: 28g | Carbohydrates: 5g | Fiber: 1g | Fat: 10g (2g saturated) | Cholesterol: 85mg | Sodium: 280mg | Potassium: 400mg

Chicken Piccata with Capers

Prep. time: 15 min | **Cook time:** 12 min | **Servings:** 4

Ingredients:

- 4 (4 oz) chicken breasts, pounded thin
- 1/4 cup almond flour
- 2 tbsp grated Parmesan cheese
- 1 tsp garlic powder
- 1/4 tsp salt
- 1/4 tsp black pepper
- 2 tbsp olive oil
- 1/4 cup chicken broth
- 2 tbsp lemon juice
- 2 tbsp capers, drained
- 2 tbsp fresh parsley, chopped

Directions:

1. Mix almond flour, Parmesan, garlic powder, salt, and pepper in a shallow dish.
2. Dip each chicken breast in the mixture, coating evenly.
3. Preheat air fryer to 380°F (193°C).
4. Place chicken in the air fryer basket and lightly spray with olive oil.
5. Cook for 6 minutes, flip, and cook for another 4-6 minutes until golden and cooked through.
6. Heat chicken broth, lemon juice, and capers in a small pan.
7. Simmer for 2-3 minutes until slightly reduced.
8. Drizzle sauce over chicken and garnish with parsley.

Serving suggestion: Serve with air-fried asparagus or zucchini noodles.

Nutrition per serving: Calories: 280 | Protein: 32g | Carbohydrates: 4g | Fiber: 1g | Fat: 15g | Cholesterol: 85mg | Sodium: 400mg | Potassium: 500mg

Chicken Bruschetta (No-Bread Version)

Prep. time: 12 min | **Cook time:** 15 min | **Servings:** 4

Ingredients:

- 4 (4 oz) chicken breasts
- 1 tsp Italian seasoning
- 1/4 tsp salt
- 1/4 tsp black pepper
- 2 tbsp olive oil

Bruschetta topping:

- 2 cups cherry tomatoes, quartered
- 1/4 cup fresh basil, chopped
- 2 cloves garlic, minced
- 1 tbsp balsamic vinegar
- 1/4 cup grated Parmesan cheese

Directions:

1. Season chicken with Italian seasoning, salt, and pepper.
2. Preheat air fryer to 380°F (193°C).
3. Place chicken in the air fryer basket and lightly spray with olive oil.
4. Cook for 6 minutes, flip, and cook for another 4-6 minutes until golden and cooked.
5. Mix tomatoes, basil, garlic, balsamic vinegar, and 1 tbsp olive oil for the topping.
6. Top cooked chicken with bruschetta mixture and sprinkle with Parmesan.
7. Return to air fryer for 1-2 minutes to warm the topping.

Serving suggestion: Serve with a side of air-fried zucchini or eggplant slices.

Nutrition per serving: Calories: 270 | Protein: 31g | Carbohydrates: 5g | Fiber: 1g | Fat: 14g | Cholesterol: 85mg | Sodium: 350mg | Potassium: 600mg

Chicken Satay with Peanut Sauce

Prep. time: 10 min + 30 marinating | **Cook time:** 10 min | **Servings:** 4

Ingredients:

Chicken Satay:

- 1 lb chicken breast, cut into strips
- 1 tbsp coconut aminos
- 1 tsp curry powder
- 1 tsp turmeric
- 1 clove garlic, minced
- 1 tbsp olive oil

Peanut Sauce:

- 1/4 cup natural peanut butter
- 2 tbsp coconut aminos
- 1 tbsp lime juice
- 1 tsp grated ginger
- 1 clove garlic, minced
- 2 tbsp water
- 1 tsp erythritol

Directions:

1. Mix coconut aminos, curry powder, turmeric, garlic, and olive oil. Marinate chicken for 30 minutes.
2. Preheat the air fryer to 375°F (190°C).
3. Thread chicken onto skewers.
4. Air fry for 8-10 minutes, turning halfway, until golden and cooked through.
5. For the sauce, whisk all ingredients until smooth.

Serving suggestion: Serve with cucumber slices and cauliflower rice.

Nutrition per serving: Calories: 290 | Protein: 32g | Carbohydrates: 6g | Fiber: 2g | Fat: 16g | Cholesterol: 85mg | Sodium: 320mg | Potassium: 550mg

Chicken and Zucchini Meatballs

Prep. time: 15 min **Cook time:** 12 min **Servings:** 4 (4 meatballs each)

Ingredients:

- 1 lb ground chicken breast
- 1 medium zucchini, grated and squeezed dry
- 1/4 cup almond flour
- 1 large egg
- 2 cloves garlic, minced
- 1 tsp dried oregano
- 1/2 tsp salt
- 1/4 tsp black pepper
- 2 tbsp grated Parmesan cheese

Directions:

1. Mix all ingredients in a large bowl until well combined.
2. Form the mixture into 16 meatballs.
3. Preheat the air fryer to 375°F (190°C).
4. Place meatballs in the air fryer basket, not overcrowding.
5. Cook for 10-12 minutes, shaking the basket halfway through.
6. Ensure internal temperature reaches 165°F (74°C).

Serving suggestion: Serve over zucchini noodles or with a side salad.

Nutrition per serving: Calories: 220 | Protein: 28g | Carbohydrates: 5g | Fiber: 2g | Fat: 11g | Cholesterol: 130mg | Sodium: 420mg | Potassium: 450mg

Chicken Tenders with Almond Flour Coating

Prep. time: 15 min **Cook time:** 12 min **Servings:** 4

Ingredients:

- 1 lb chicken tenders
- 1 cup almond flour
- 1/4 cup grated Parmesan cheese
- 1 tsp paprika
- 1 tsp garlic powder
- 1/2 tsp salt
- 1/4 tsp black pepper
- 2 large eggs
- 1 tbsp olive oil spray

Directions:

1. Mix almond flour, Parmesan, paprika, garlic powder, salt, and pepper in a shallow dish.
2. Beat eggs in another shallow dish.
3. Dip each chicken tender in egg, then coat with almond flour.
4. Preheat air fryer to 380°F (193°C).
5. Place coated tenders in the air fryer basket without overcrowding.
6. Spray lightly with olive oil.
7. Cook for 6 minutes, flip, spray again, and cook for another 5-6 minutes until golden and crispy.

Serving suggestion: Serve with air-fried vegetables or a mixed green salad.

Nutrition per serving: Calories: 340 | Protein: 34g | Carbohydrates: 7g | Fiber: 3g | Fat: 21g | Cholesterol: 155mg | Sodium: 420mg | Potassium: 400mg

Curry-Spiced Chicken Thighs

Prep. time: 10 min | **Cook time:** 20 min | **Servings:** 4

Ingredients:

- 4 bone-in, skin-on chicken thighs (about 1.5 lbs)
- 2 tbsp olive oil
- 2 tsp curry powder
- 1 tsp turmeric
- 1 tsp garlic powder
- 1/2 tsp ground ginger
- 1/2 tsp salt
- 1/4 tsp black pepper
- 1 lime, cut into wedges

Directions:

1. In a small bowl, mix olive oil, curry powder, turmeric, garlic powder, ginger, salt, and pepper.
2. Rub the spice mixture all over the chicken thighs, including under the skin.
3. Preheat the air fryer to 380°F (193°C).
4. Place chicken thighs in the air fryer basket, skin side up, not overcrowding.
5. Cook for 15 minutes, then flip and cook for another 5-7 minutes until skin is crispy and internal temperature reaches 165°F (74°C).
6. Let rest for 5 minutes before serving.

Serving suggestion: Serve with cauliflower rice and steamed green vegetables. Squeeze lime juice over the chicken before eating.

Nutrition per serving: Calories: 320 | Protein: 28g | Carbohydrates: 2g | Fiber: 1g | Fat: 23g | Cholesterol: 145mg | Sodium: 380mg | Potassium: 350mg

Greek Yogurt Marinated Chicken Skewers

Prep. time: 10 min + 2 h marinating | **Cook time:** 12 min | **Servings:** 4

Ingredients:

- 1 lb chicken breast, cut into 1-inch cubes
- 1/2 cup plain Greek yogurt
- 2 tbsp lemon juice
- 2 cloves garlic, minced
- 1 tsp dried oregano
- 1 tsp dried rosemary
- 1/2 tsp salt
- 1/4 tsp black pepper
- 1 medium zucchini, cut into 1-inch pieces
- 1 red bell pepper, cut into 1-inch pieces

Directions:

1. Mix a bowl of yogurt, lemon juice, garlic, oregano, rosemary, salt, and pepper.
2. Add chicken, coat well, and marinate for 2 hours in the refrigerator.
3. Preheat the air fryer to 375°F (190°C).
4. Thread chicken, zucchini, and bell pepper onto skewers.
5. Place skewers in the air fryer basket, not overcrowding.
6. Cook for 10-12 minutes, turning halfway, until chicken is cooked through.

Serving suggestion: Serve with a side of tzatziki sauce and a Greek salad.

Nutrition per serving: Calories: 220 | Protein: 32g | Carbohydrates: 6g | Fiber: 1g | Fat: 8g | Cholesterol: 85mg | Sodium: 380mg | Potassium: 550mg

Beef

Beef and Broccoli Stir-fry

🥣 **Prep. time:** 15 min   🕐 **Cook time:** 13 min   🍴 **Servings:** 4

Ingredients:

- 1 lb lean beef sirloin, sliced thin
- 4 cups broccoli florets
- 1 red bell pepper, sliced
- 2 tbsp olive oil
- 3 tbsp low-sodium soy sauce
- 1 tbsp rice vinegar
- 1 tbsp grated fresh ginger
- 2 cloves garlic, minced
- 1 tsp sesame oil
- 1 tbsp erythritol or monk fruit sweetener
- 1/4 tsp xanthan gum
- 1 tbsp sesame seeds

Directions:

1. Mix a bowl of soy sauce, vinegar, ginger, garlic, sesame oil, and sweetener.
2. Toss beef slices with half the sauce mixture.
3. Preheat the air fryer to 400°F (200°C).
4. Air fry broccoli and bell pepper with 1 tbsp olive oil for 5 minutes, shaking halfway.
5. Remove vegetables and add beef to the basket. Air fry for 4-5 minutes, shaking halfway.
6. Add vegetables back to the basket with beef, and air fry for 2-3 more minutes.
7. Heat the remaining sauce in a small pan; add xanthan gum to thicken slightly.
8. Toss cooked beef and vegetables with thickened sauce.
9. Sprinkle with sesame seeds before serving.

Serving suggestion: Serve over cauliflower rice or with a cucumber salad.

Nutrition per serving: Calories: 280 | Protein: 29g | Carbohydrates: 10g | Fiber: 3g | Fat: 15g (4g saturated) | Cholesterol: 70mg | Sodium: 400mg | Potassium: 650mg

Stuffed Bell Peppers with Ground Beef

🥣 **Prep. time:** 20 min   🕐 **Cook time:** 17 min   🍴 **Servings:** 4

Ingredients:

- 4 medium bell peppers, any color
- 1 lb lean ground beef (93% lean)
- 1/2 cup riced cauliflower
- 1/4 cup diced onion
- 1 clove garlic, minced
- 1 can (14.5 oz) diced tomatoes, drained
- 1 tsp Italian seasoning
- 1/2 tsp salt
- 1/4 tsp black pepper
- 1/2 cup shredded mozzarella cheese
- 2 tbsp chopped fresh parsley

Directions:

1. Cut tops off peppers and remove seeds. Set aside.
2. Mix ground beef, cauliflower rice, onion, garlic, tomatoes, Italian seasoning, salt, and pepper in a bowl.
3. Stuff peppers with beef mixture.
4. Preheat the air fryer to 350°F (175°C).
5. Place stuffed peppers in the air fryer basket, standing upright.
6. Cook for 12-15 minutes until beef is cooked and peppers tender.
7. Sprinkle cheese on top and cook for 2-3 more minutes until cheese melts.
8. Garnish with parsley before serving.

Serving suggestion: Pair with a mixed green salad or steamed non-starchy vegetables.

Nutrition per serving (1 stuffed pepper): Calories: 310 | Protein: 28g | Carbohydrates: 12g | Fiber: 3g | Fat: 18g (8g saturated) | Cholesterol: 85mg | Sodium: 550mg | Potassium: 600mg

Marinated Flank Steak with Grilled Veggies

Prep. time: 15 min + 2 h marinating | **Cook time:** 17 min | **Servings:** 4

Ingredients:

- 1 lb flank steak
- 2 tbsp olive oil
- 2 tbsp balsamic vinegar
- 2 cloves garlic, minced
- 1 tsp dried rosemary
- 1/2 tsp salt
- 1/4 tsp black pepper
- 1 medium zucchini, sliced
- 1 red bell pepper, sliced
- 1 yellow bell pepper, sliced
- 1 small red onion, sliced

Directions:

1. Mix olive oil, balsamic vinegar, garlic, rosemary, salt, and pepper in a bowl.
2. Place flank steak in a zip lock bag and add half the marinade. Refrigerate for 2 hours.
3. Toss vegetables with remaining marinade.
4. Preheat the air fryer to 400°F (200°C).
5. Air fry vegetables for 8-10 minutes, shaking basket halfway through.
6. Remove vegetables and add flank steak to the basket.
7. Air fry steak for 5-6 minutes per side for medium-rare (adjust time for desired doneness).
8. Let steak rest for 5 minutes before slicing against the grain.
9. Serve sliced steak with air-fried vegetables.

Serving suggestion: Pair with a side of mixed greens or cucumber salad.

Nutrition per serving: Calories: 280 | Protein: 29g | Carbohydrates: 8g | Fiber: 2g | Fat: 15g (4g saturated) | Cholesterol: 70mg | Sodium: 350mg | Potassium: 600mg

Garlic-Herb Crusted Roast Beef

Prep. time: 10 min | **Cook time:** 28 min | **Servings:** 4

Ingredients:

- 1.5 lbs beef eye of round roast
- 2 tbsp olive oil
- 4 cloves garlic, minced
- 1 tbsp fresh rosemary, chopped
- 1 tbsp fresh thyme, chopped
- 1 tsp salt
- 1/2 tsp black pepper
- 1 tsp Dijon mustard

Directions:

1. Mix olive oil, garlic, rosemary, thyme, salt, pepper, and mustard in a bowl.
2. Rub mixture all over the beef roast.
3. Preheat the air fryer to 390°F (200°C).
4. Place roast in an air fryer basket.
5. Cook for 25-30 minutes, flipping halfway through, for medium-rare (internal temperature 135°F/57°C). Adjust time for desired doneness.
6. Let rest for 10 minutes before slicing.

Serving suggestion: Pair with air-fried asparagus or a mixed green salad.

Nutrition per serving: Calories: 290 | Protein: 36g | Carbohydrates: 1g | Fiber: 0g | Fat: 16g (4g saturated) | Cholesterol: 95mg | Sodium: 380mg | Potassium: 500mg

Ground Beef Lettuce Wraps with Avocado Salsa

Prep. time: 15 min **Cook time:** 12 min **Servings:** 4

Ingredients:

- 1 lb lean ground beef (93% lean)
- 1 tbsp olive oil
- 2 cloves garlic, minced
- 1 tsp ground cumin
- 1 tsp smoked paprika
- 1/2 tsp chili powder
- 1/4 tsp salt
- 1/4 tsp black pepper

- 1 ripe avocado, diced
- 1/2 cup diced tomatoes
- 1/4 cup diced red onion
- 2 tbsp chopped cilantro
- 1 tbsp lime juice
- Salt to taste

Directions:

1. Mix ground beef with garlic, cumin, paprika, chili powder, salt, and pepper.
2. Preheat air fryer to 380°F (193°C).
3. Spread the beef mixture evenly in the air fryer basket.
4. Cook for 8-10 minutes, stirring halfway through, until beef is browned and cooked.
5. While beef cooks, prepare avocado salsa by mixing the ingredients in a bowl.
6. Serve cooked beef in lettuce leaves, topped with avocado salsa.

Serving suggestion: Pair with a side of cucumber slices or bell pepper strips.

Nutrition per serving (2 lettuce wraps with beef and salsa): Calories: 310 | Protein: 26g | Carbohydrates: 8g | Fiber: 4g | Fat: 20g (5g saturated) | Cholesterol: 70mg | Sodium: 280mg | Potassium: 650mg

Pepper-Steak Skewers

Prep. time: 10 min + 30 min marinating **Cook time:** 12 min **Servings:** 4

Ingredients:

- 1 lb beef sirloin, cut into 1-inch cubes
- 1 red bell pepper, cut into 1-inch pieces
- 1 green bell pepper, cut into 1-inch pieces
- 1 medium onion, cut into 1-inch pieces
- 2 tbsp olive oil
- 2 tbsp balsamic vinegar
- 2 cloves garlic, minced
- 1 tsp dried oregano
- 1 tsp ground black pepper
- 1/2 tsp salt

Directions:

1. Mix olive oil, balsamic vinegar, garlic, oregano, black pepper, and salt in a bowl.
2. Toss beef cubes in marinade and refrigerate for 30 minutes.
3. Thread marinated beef, bell peppers, and onions alternately onto skewers.
4. Preheat the air fryer to 400°F (200°C).
5. Place skewers in the air fryer basket, ensuring they don't touch.
6. Cook for 10-12 minutes, turning skewers halfway through, until beef is cooked to the desired doneness.

Serving suggestion: Serve over a bed of mixed greens or with a side of roasted zucchini.

Nutrition per serving (2 skewers): Calories: 280 | Protein: 28g | Carbohydrates: 8g | Fiber: 2g | Fat: 16g (4g saturated) | Cholesterol: 70mg | Sodium: 330mg | Potassium: 550mg

Balsamic-Glazed Top Sirloin Steak with Asparagus

Prep. time: 15 min   **Cook time:** 15 min   **Servings:** 4

Ingredients:

- 1 lb top sirloin steak, trimmed of excess fat and cut into 4 portions
- 1 lb asparagus, trimmed
- 2 tbsp balsamic vinegar
- 1 tbsp olive oil
- 1 tsp Dijon mustard
- 2 cloves garlic, minced
- 1 tsp dried rosemary
- Salt and pepper to taste
- 1 tsp erythritol (optional for added sweetness)

Directions:

1. In a small bowl, mix balsamic vinegar, olive oil, Dijon mustard, minced garlic, rosemary, salt, pepper, and erythritol (if using) to create the marinade.
2. Place steak portions in a shallow dish and pour half the marinade over them. Turn to coat evenly. Let marinate for 10 minutes at room temperature.
3. Preheat the air fryer to 400°F (200°C).
4. Divide asparagus into 4 bundles. Wrap each bundle with kitchen twine.
5. Place marinated steak and asparagus bundles in the air fryer basket, ensuring they're not overcrowded.
6. Cook the steak for 8-10 minutes for medium-rare, flipping halfway through. Adjust the time to the desired doneness.
7. Remove steak and let rest. Continue cooking asparagus for 2-3 more minutes until tender-crisp.
8. Brush the remaining marinade over the steak and asparagus before serving.

Serving suggestion: Serve each steak portion with an asparagus bundle. If desired, pair it with a small side salad of mixed greens.

Nutritional Information (per serving): Calories: 290 | Protein: 35g | Carbohydrates: 6g | Fiber: 3g | Net Carbs: 3g | Fat: 15g | Cholesterol: 70mg | Sodium: 180mg | Potassium: 700mg

Homemade Beef Meatballs

Prep. time: 15 min   **Cook time:** 12 min   **Servings:** 4 (4 meatballs per serving)

Ingredients:

- 1 lb lean ground beef (90% lean)
- 1/4 cup ground flaxseed
- 1 large egg
- 1/4 cup grated Parmesan cheese
- 1/4 cup finely chopped onion
- 2 cloves garlic, minced
- 1 tsp dried oregano
- 1 tsp dried basil
- 1/4 cup chopped fresh parsley
- 1/2 tsp salt
- 1/4 tsp black pepper
- 1 tbsp olive oil (for brushing)

Directions:

1. Mix all ingredients except olive oil in a large bowl until well combined.
2. Form 16 evenly sized meatballs.
3. Preheat the air fryer to 375°F (190°C).
4. Lightly brush the air fryer basket with olive oil.
5. Place meatballs in a basket, leaving space between each. Cook in batches if needed.
6. Air fry for 10-12 minutes, shaking basket or turning meatballs halfway through.
7. Ensure internal temperature reaches 160°F (71°C).

Serving suggestion: Serve with roasted vegetables or over cauliflower rice. Mix 1/2 cup unsweetened marinara with 1 tsp Italian herbs for a sauce.

Nutritional Information (per serving - 4 meatballs): Calories: 290 | Protein: 29g | Carbohydrates: 3g | Fiber: 2g | Net Carbs: 1g | Fat: 19g | Cholesterol: 120mg | Sodium: 450mg | Potassium: 400mg

Zesty Lime & Chili Flank Steak Fajitas

Prep. time: 20 min + 30 min marinating **Cook time:** 15 min **Servings:** 4

Ingredients:

- 1 lb flank steak, sliced thinly against the grain
- 2 bell peppers (mixed colors), sliced
- 1 medium onion, sliced
- 2 tbsp olive oil
- 2 limes, juiced
- 2 cloves garlic, minced
- 1 tbsp chili powder
- 1 tsp ground cumin
- 1/2 tsp smoked paprika
- 1/2 tsp salt
- 1/4 tsp black pepper

Directions:

1. Mix olive oil, lime juice, garlic, and spices in a bowl.
2. Marinate sliced steak in the mixture for 30 minutes in the refrigerator.
3. Preheat the air fryer to 400°F (200°C).
4. Cook marinated steak in an air fryer basket for 5 minutes.
5. Add peppers and onions and drizzle with the remaining marinade.
6. Cook for 5-7 minutes more, shaking basket halfway through.

Serving suggestion: Serve over cauliflower rice or in lettuce wraps. Top with avocado slices and cilantro.

Nutritional Information (per serving): Calories: 290 | Protein: 28g | Carbohydrates: 8g | Fiber: 2g | Net Carbs: 6g | Fat: 17g | Cholesterol: 70mg | Sodium: 380mg | Potassium: 600mg

Sesame-Ginger Beef Stir-Fry

Prep. time: 20 min + 30 min marinating **Cook time:** 15 min **Servings:** 4

Ingredients:

- 1 lb lean beef sirloin, sliced thinly
- 2 cups broccoli florets
- 1 red bell pepper, sliced
- 1 cup snap peas
- 2 tbsp sesame oil
- 2 tbsp low-sodium soy sauce
- 1 tbsp rice vinegar
- 1 tbsp grated fresh ginger
- 2 cloves garlic, minced
- 1 tbsp erythritol
- 1 tsp sesame seeds

Directions:

1. Mix sesame oil, soy sauce, rice vinegar, ginger, garlic, and erythritol in a bowl.
2. Marinate beef in half the mixture for 30 minutes in the refrigerator.
3. Preheat the air fryer to 375°F (190°C).
4. Cook marinated beef in an air fryer basket for 5 minutes.
5. Add vegetables and remaining marinade. Cook for 7-8 minutes, shaking basket halfway through.
6. Sprinkle with sesame seeds before serving.

Serving suggestion: Serve over cauliflower rice or shirataki noodles. Garnish with sliced green onions.

Nutritional Information (per serving): Calories: 280 | Protein: 30g | Carbohydrates: 10g | Fiber: 3g | Net Carbs: 7g | Fat: 15g | Cholesterol: 65mg | Sodium: 350mg | Potassium: 650mg

Cheesy Stuffed Mushrooms with Minced Beef

Prep. time: 15 min | **Cook time:** 12 min | **Servings:** 4

Ingredients:

- 12 large white mushrooms
- 8 oz lean ground beef (90% lean)
- 1/4 cup finely chopped onion
- 1 clove garlic, minced
- 1/4 cup grated Parmesan cheese
- 1/4 cup shredded mozzarella cheese
- 2 tbsp chopped fresh parsley
- 1 tsp olive oil
- 1/2 tsp dried oregano
- 1/4 tsp salt
- 1/8 tsp black pepper

Directions:

1. Remove stems from mushrooms and finely chop them.
2. In a skillet, cook beef, chopped stems, onion, and garlic until beef is browned.
3. Remove from heat; stir in cheeses, parsley, oregano, salt, and pepper.
4. Preheat the air fryer to 375°F (190°C).
5. Brush mushroom caps with olive oil and fill with beef mixture.
6. Place stuffed mushrooms in an air fryer basket.
7. Cook for 10-12 minutes until mushrooms are tender and cheese is melted.

Serving suggestion: Serve as an appetizer or with a side salad for a light meal.

Nutritional Information (per serving - 3 mushrooms): Calories: 180 | Protein: 18g | Carbohydrates: 5g | Fiber: 1g | Net Carbs: 4g | Fat: 11g | Cholesterol: 45mg | Sodium: 320mg | Potassium: 450mg

Hearty Grilled Aubergine & Ground Beef Lasagna

Prep. time: 20 min | **Cook time:** 25 min | **Servings:** 4

Ingredients:

- 2 medium aubergines (eggplants), sliced lengthwise 1/4 inch thick
- 1 lb lean ground beef (90% lean)
- 1 cup sugar-free marinara sauce
- 1 cup ricotta cheese
- 1/2 cup grated Parmesan cheese
- 1 cup shredded mozzarella cheese
- 1 egg
- 1 tsp dried oregano
- 1 tsp dried basil, 2 cloves garlic, minced
- Salt and pepper to taste, olive oil spray

Directions:

1. Preheat the air fryer to 400°F (200°C).
2. Spray aubergine slices with olive oil and season with salt and pepper. Air fry for 5 minutes, flip, and cook for 3 more minutes. Set aside.
3. Brown ground beef with garlic in a skillet. Add marinara sauce and simmer for 5 minutes.
4. Mix ricotta, egg, half the Parmesan, oregano, and basil in a bowl.
5. In a square baking dish that fits your air fryer:
    - Layer aubergine slices
    - Spread half the beef mixture
    - Add half the ricotta mixture
    - Sprinkle 1/3 of mozzarella
    - Repeat layers
    - Top with remaining mozzarella and Parmesan
6. Place in air fryer basket and cook at 350°F (175°C) for 15-18 minutes until cheese is bubbly and golden.

Serving suggestion: Pair with a side salad of mixed greens.

Nutritional Information (per serving): Calories: 420 | Protein: 38g | Carbohydrates: 12g | Fiber: 5g | Net Carbs: 7g | Fat: 25g | Cholesterol: 140mg | Sodium: 650mg | Potassium: 800mg

Lamb

Rosemary and Thyme-Infused Lamb Chops

Prep. time: 10 min + 30 min marinating | **Cook time:** 12 min | **Servings:** 4

Ingredients:

- 8 lamb loin chops (about 4 oz each)
- 2 tbsp olive oil
- 2 cloves garlic, minced
- 2 tsp fresh rosemary, finely chopped
- 2 tsp fresh thyme leaves
- 1 tsp lemon zest
- 1/2 tsp salt
- 1/4 tsp black pepper

Directions:

1. Mix olive oil, garlic, rosemary, thyme, lemon zest, salt, and pepper in a bowl.
2. Coat lamb chops with the mixture and marinate for 30 minutes at room temperature.
3. Preheat the air fryer to 375°F (190°C).
4. Place lamb chops in the air fryer basket in a single layer.
5. Cook for 6 minutes, then flip and cook for another 4-6 minutes for medium-rare.
6. Let rest for 5 minutes before serving.

Serving suggestion: Serve with roasted asparagus or a mixed green salad.

Nutritional Information (per serving - 2 lamb chops): Calories: 320 | Protein: 28g | Carbohydrates: 1g | Fiber: 0g | Net Carbs: 1g | Fat: 23g | Cholesterol: 95mg | Sodium: 340mg | Potassium: 350mg

Mediterranean Lamb Kebabs with Tzatziki

Prep. time: 20 min + 2 hours marinating | **Cook time:** 12 min | **Servings:** 4

Ingredients:

For the kebabs:
- 1 lb lean lamb, cut into 1-inch cubes
- 1 zucchini, cut into chunks
- 1 red onion, cut into chunks
- 1 red bell pepper, cut into chunks
- 2 tbsp olive oil
- 2 cloves garlic, minced
- 1 tbsp lemon juice
- 1 tsp dried oregano
- 1 tsp ground cumin
- 1/2 tsp salt
- 1/4 tsp black pepper

For the tzatziki sauce:
- 1 cup Greek yogurt
- 1/2 cucumber, grated and drained
- 1 clove garlic, minced
- 1 tbsp lemon juice
- 1 tbsp fresh dill, chopped
- Salt and pepper to taste

Directions:

1. Mix olive oil, garlic, lemon juice, oregano, cumin, salt, and pepper in a bowl.
2. Add lamb cubes to the marinade, coat well, and refrigerate for 2 hours.
3. Meanwhile, prepare tzatziki sauce by mixing all sauce ingredients. Refrigerate.
4. Preheat the air fryer to 375°F (190°C).
5. Thread marinated lamb and vegetables onto skewers.
6. Place skewers in the air fryer basket, ensuring they don't touch.
7. Cook for 10-12 minutes, turning halfway through, until lamb is cooked and vegetables are tender.

Serving suggestion: Serve kebabs with tzatziki sauce and mixed greens.

Nutritional Information (per serving): Calories: 310 | Protein: 28g | Carbohydrates: 10g | Fiber: 2g | Net Carbs: 8g | Fat: 18g | Cholesterol: 85mg | Sodium: 420mg | Potassium: 550mg

Shepherd's Pie with Cauliflower Mash

Prep. time: 20 min | **Cook time:** 25 min | **Servings:** 4

Ingredients:

- 1 lb lean ground lamb
- 1 cup mixed vegetables (carrots, peas, celery)
- 1/2 onion, diced
- 2 cloves garlic, minced
- 1/2 cup beef broth
- 1 tbsp tomato paste
- 1 tsp dried thyme
- 1/2 tsp dried rosemary
- Salt and pepper to taste

For the cauliflower mash:
- 1 medium cauliflower head, cut into florets
- 2 tbsp butter
- 1/4 cup grated Parmesan cheese
- Salt and pepper to taste

Directions:

1. In a skillet, brown lamb with onion and garlic. Add vegetables, broth, tomato paste, and herbs. Simmer for 10 minutes.
2. Meanwhile, steam cauliflower until tender. Mash with butter, Parmesan, salt, and pepper.
3. Preheat the air fryer to 375°F (190°C).
4. Transfer the lamb mixture to an air fryer-safe dish. Top with cauliflower mash.
5. Air fry for 15 minutes until top is golden and crispy.

Serving suggestion: Serve hot, garnished with fresh parsley if desired.

Nutritional Information (per serving): Calories: 350 | Protein: 28g | Carbohydrates: 12g | Fiber: 4g | Net Carbs: 8g | Fat: 22g | Cholesterol: 95mg | Sodium: 380mg | Potassium: 700mg

Cumin Spiced Lamb Skewers with Grilled Veggies

Prep. time: 20 min + 2 hours marinating | **Cook time:** 15 min | **Servings:** 4

Ingredients:

For the lamb skewers:
- 1 lb lean lamb, cut into 1-inch cubes
- 2 tbsp olive oil
- 2 tsp ground cumin
- 1 tsp smoked paprika
- 1 tsp garlic powder
- 1/2 tsp salt
- 1/4 tsp black pepper

For the grilled veggies:
- 1 zucchini, sliced
- 1 red bell pepper, chunked
- 1 red onion, chunked
- 1 tbsp olive oil
- Salt and pepper to taste

Directions:

1. Mix olive oil, cumin, paprika, garlic powder, salt, and pepper. Coat lamb cubes and marinate for 2 hours.
2. Preheat the air fryer to 375°F (190°C).
3. Thread lamb onto skewers. Place in air fryer basket.
4. Cook for 10-12 minutes, turning halfway through.
5. Toss vegetables with olive oil, salt, and pepper.
6. After removing the lamb, air fry vegetables at 375°F for 5-7 minutes, shaking the basket halfway through.

Serving suggestion: Serve lamb skewers over grilled veggies with a dollop of Greek yogurt.

Nutritional Information (per serving): Calories: 320 | Protein: 28g | Carbohydrates: 8g | Fiber: 2g | Net Carbs: 6g | Fat: 20g | Cholesterol: 85mg | Sodium: 400mg | Potassium: 600mg

Greek Style Stuffed Bell Peppers with Ground Lamb

Prep. time: 20 min | **Cook time:** 20 min | **Servings:** 4

Ingredients:

- 4 large bell peppers, any color
- 1 lb lean ground lamb
- 1/2 cup crumbled feta cheese
- 1/4 cup diced onion
- 1 clove garlic, minced
- 1/4 cup chopped fresh parsley
- 1 tsp dried oregano
- 1 tbsp olive oil
- 1/4 cup low-sodium beef broth
- Salt and pepper to taste

Directions:

1. Cut tops off peppers and remove seeds. Set aside.
2. Mix lamb, feta, onion, garlic, parsley, oregano, salt, and pepper in a bowl.
3. Stuff peppers with lamb mixture.
4. Preheat the air fryer to 350°F (175°C).
5. Place stuffed peppers in an air fryer basket. Drizzle with olive oil.
6. Cook for 15-20 minutes, until peppers are tender and lamb is cooked.
7. Pour 1 tbsp beef broth over each pepper halfway through cooking.

Serving suggestion: Serve with a side of Greek salad or tzatziki sauce.

Nutritional Information (per serving): Calories: 350 | Protein: 28g | Carbohydrates: 10g | Fiber: 3g | Net Carbs: 7g | Fat: 23g | Cholesterol: 90mg | Sodium: 380mg | Potassium: 550mg

Moroccan-Inspired Lamb Shanks

Prep. time: 15 min | **Cook time:** 45 min | **Servings:** 4

Ingredients:

- 4 lamb shanks (about 12 oz each)
- 1 tbsp olive oil
- 1 tsp ground cumin
- 1 tsp ground coriander
- 1 tsp smoked paprika
- 1/2 tsp ground cinnamon
- 1/4 tsp ground ginger
- 2 cloves garlic, minced
- 1 lemon, juiced
- Salt and pepper to taste
- 1/4 cup low-sodium chicken broth
- 1 cup mixed vegetables (carrots, zucchini, bell peppers)

Directions:

1. Mix olive oil, spices, garlic, and lemon juice. Rub over lamb shanks.
2. Preheat the air fryer to 350°F (175°C).
3. Place lamb shanks in an air fryer basket. Cook for 20 minutes.
4. Turn the shanks and add broth and vegetables. Cook for 20-25 more minutes until tender.
5. Let rest for 5 minutes before serving.

Serving suggestion: Serve with cauliflower "couscous" or roasted vegetables.

Nutritional Information (per serving): Calories: 380 | Protein: 35g | Carbohydrates: 5g | Fiber: 2g | Net Carbs: 3g | Fat: 25g | Cholesterol: 110mg | Sodium: 120mg | Potassium: 600mg

Skillet-style Ground Lamb and Eggplant Moussaka

Prep. time: 20 min **Cook time:** 30 min **Servings:** 4

Ingredients:

- 1 lb lean ground lamb
- 1 large eggplant, sliced 1/4 inch thick
- 1/2 cup diced onion
- 2 cloves garlic, minced
- 1/4 cup tomato paste
- 1 tsp dried oregano
- 1 tsp ground cinnamon
- 1/4 cup crumbled feta cheese
- 1/4 cup Greek yogurt
- 1 egg
- 2 tbsp olive oil
- Salt and pepper to taste

Directions:

1. Preheat the air fryer to 375°F (190°C).
2. Brush eggplant slices with 1 tbsp olive oil. Air fry for 10 minutes, flipping halfway.
3. In a skillet, brown lamb with onion and garlic. Add tomato paste, oregano, and cinnamon.
4. Mix feta, yogurt, and egg for topping in a bowl.
5. In an air fryer-safe dish, layer eggplant and lamb mixture. Pour topping over.
6. Air fry at 350°F (175°C) for 15-20 minutes until top is golden.

Serving suggestion: Serve with a side of mixed greens.

Nutritional Information (per serving): Calories: 380 | Protein: 28g | Carbohydrates: 12g | Fiber: 4g | Net Carbs: 8g | Fat: 26g | Cholesterol: 115mg | Sodium: 350mg | Potassium: 700mg

Herb-Crusted Rack of Lamb with Grilled Asparagus

Prep. time: 15 min **Cook time:** 20 min **Servings:** 4

Ingredients:

- 1 rack of lamb (8 ribs, about 1.5 lbs)
- 2 tbsp Dijon mustard
- 2 tbsp fresh rosemary, finely chopped
- 2 tbsp fresh thyme leaves
- 2 cloves garlic, minced
- 1 tbsp olive oil
- Salt and pepper to taste
- 1 lb asparagus spears, trimmed

Directions:

1. Mix Dijon mustard, rosemary, thyme, garlic, salt, and pepper.
2. Coat lamb rack with herb mixture.
3. Preheat the air fryer to 375°F (190°C).
4. Place lamb in an air fryer basket, fat side up. Cook for 15 minutes for medium-rare.
5. Remove lamb, let rest.
6. Toss asparagus with olive oil, salt, and pepper.
7. Air fry asparagus at 400°F (200°C) for 5-7 minutes, shaking basket halfway.

Serving suggestion: Slice lamb between ribs and serve with grilled asparagus.

Nutritional Information (per serving): Calories: 350 | Protein: 32g | Carbohydrates: 5g | Fiber: 2g | Net Carbs: 3g | Fat: 23g | Cholesterol: 95mg | Sodium: 180mg | Potassium: 500mg

Garlic & Lemongrass Leg of Lamb

Prep. time: 20 min + 2 hours marinating | **Cook time:** 40 min | **Servings:** 4

Ingredients:

- 2 lbs boneless leg of lamb
- 4 cloves garlic, minced
- 2 stalks lemongrass, finely chopped
- 2 tbsp olive oil
- 1 tbsp fresh ginger, grated
- 1 tbsp low-sodium soy sauce
- 1 tsp erythritol (optional for sweetness)
- Salt and pepper to taste

Directions:

1. Mix garlic, lemongrass, olive oil, ginger, soy sauce, erythritol, salt, and pepper.
2. Rub mixture over lamb. Marinate for 2 hours in the refrigerator.
3. Preheat the air fryer to 375°F (190°C).
4. Place lamb in an air fryer basket. Cook for 20 minutes.
5. Flip lamb and cook for 15-20 minutes until internal temperature reaches 145°F (63°C) for medium-rare.
6. Let rest for 10 minutes before slicing.

Serving suggestion: Serve with air-fried vegetables like zucchini or bell peppers.

Nutritional Information (per serving): Calories: 320 | Protein: 38g | Carbohydrates: 2g | Fiber: 0g | Net Carbs: 2g | Fat: 18g | Cholesterol: 110mg | Sodium: 200mg | Potassium: 550mg

Lamb Meatballs Stuffed with Feta Cheese

Prep. time: 20 min | **Cook time:** 15 min | **Servings:** 4

Ingredients:

For meatballs:

- 1 lb ground lamb
- 1/4 cup almond flour
- 1 egg
- 2 cloves garlic, minced
- 1 tsp dried oregano
- 1/2 tsp salt
- 1/4 tsp black pepper
- 2 oz feta cheese, cubed

For sauce:

- 1 cup sugar-free tomato sauce
- 1 tsp dried basil
- 1/4 tsp garlic powder

Directions:

1. Mix lamb, almond flour, egg, garlic, oregano, salt, and pepper.
2. Form 12 meatballs, stuffing each with a feta cube.
3. Preheat the air fryer to 375°F (190°C).
4. Air fry meatballs for 10 minutes, shaking basket halfway through.
5. Mix tomato sauce with basil and garlic powder in an air fryer-safe dish.
6. Add meatballs to sauce and air fry for 5 more minutes at 350°F (175°C).

Serving suggestion: Serve over zucchini noodles or with a side of roasted vegetables.

Nutritional Information (per serving - 3 meatballs): Calories: 340 | Protein: 28g | Carbohydrates: 6g | Fiber: 2g | Net Carbs: 4g | Fat: 24g | Cholesterol: 115mg | Sodium: 580mg | Potassium: 450mg

Spinach & Minced Lamb Stuffed Zucchini Boats

Prep. time: 20 min | **Cook time:** 15 min | **Servings:** 4

Ingredients:

- 4 medium zucchinis
- 1/2 lb lean ground lamb
- 2 cups fresh spinach, chopped
- 1/4 cup onion, finely diced
- 2 cloves garlic, minced
- 1/4 cup crumbled feta cheese
- 1 tbsp olive oil
- 1 tsp dried oregano
- 1/2 tsp ground cumin
- Salt and pepper to taste

Directions:

1. Cut zucchini in half lengthwise. Scoop out centers, leaving 1/4-inch-thick shells.
2. Preheat the air fryer to 375°F (190°C).
3. In a skillet, cook lamb, onion, and garlic until lamb is browned.
4. Add spinach, oregano, cumin, salt, and pepper. Cook until spinach wilts.
5. Stir in feta cheese.
6. Fill zucchini boats with lamb mixture.
7. Brush zucchini with olive oil.
8. Air fry for 12-15 minutes until the zucchini is tender and the filling is hot.

Serving suggestion: Serve with a side of mixed greens or cucumber salad.

Nutritional Information (per serving - 2 zucchini boats): Calories: 250 | Protein: 18g | Carbohydrates: 8g | Fiber: 2g | Net Carbs: 6g | Fat: 17g | Cholesterol: 55mg | Sodium: 280mg | Potassium: 650mg

Middle Eastern Kofta Wraps

Prep. time: 15 min | **Cook time:** 12 min | **Servings:** 4

Ingredients:

For kofta:
- 1 lb lean ground lamb
- 1/4 cup finely chopped onion
- 2 cloves garlic, minced
- 2 tbsp chopped fresh parsley
- 1 tsp ground cumin
- 1 tsp ground coriander
- 1/2 tsp cinnamon
- 1/4 tsp allspice
- Salt and pepper to taste

For serving:
- 4 large lettuce leaves
- 1/2 cup tzatziki sauce (Greek yogurt)
- 1/2 cucumber, sliced
- 1/4 red onion, thinly sliced

Directions:

1. Mix all kofta ingredients in a bowl.
2. Form the mixture into 8 oval-shaped patties.
3. Preheat the air fryer to 375°F (190°C).
4. Place patties in the air fryer basket, ensuring they don't overlap.
5. Cook for 10-12 minutes, flipping halfway through, until internal temperature reaches 160°F (71°C).

Serving suggestion: Place 2 kofta patties in each lettuce leaf. Top with tzatziki, cucumber, and red onion.

Nutritional Information (per serving - 2 kofta patties with toppings): Calories: 300 | Protein: 25g | Carbohydrates: 7g | Fiber: 2g | Net Carbs: 5g | Fat: 20g | Cholesterol: 75mg | Sodium: 200mg | Potassium: 400mg

Grilled Ratatouille Salad & Marinated Lamb Cutlets

Prep. time: 20 min + 1 hour marinating **Cook time:** 20 min **Servings:** 4

Ingredients:

For lamb cutlets:
- 8 lamb cutlets (about 1.5 lbs)
- 2 tbsp olive oil
- 2 cloves garlic, minced
- 1 tbsp fresh rosemary, chopped
- 1 tbsp lemon juice
- Salt and pepper to taste

For ratatouille salad:
- 1 small eggplant, cubed
- 1 zucchini, sliced
- 1 red bell pepper, chunked
- 1 yellow bell pepper, chunked
- 1 red onion, cut into wedges
- 2 tbsp olive oil
- 1 tsp dried herbs, de Provence
Salt and pepper to taste

Directions:

1. Mix olive oil, garlic, rosemary, lemon juice, salt, and pepper. Marinate lamb cutlets for 1 hour.
2. Preheat the air fryer to 400°F (200°C).
3. Toss ratatouille vegetables with olive oil, herbs, salt, and pepper.
4. Air fry vegetables for 12-15 minutes, shaking basket halfway through.
5. Remove vegetables. Air fry lamb cutlets at 375°F (190°C) for 6-8 minutes, flipping halfway.
6. Toss cooked vegetables together to create the ratatouille salad.

Serving suggestion: Serve lamb cutlets alongside the warm ratatouille salad.

Nutritional Information (per serving): Calories: 380 | Protein: 28g | Carbohydrates: 12g | Fiber: 4g | Net Carbs: 8g | Fat: 26g | Cholesterol: 85mg | Sodium: 180mg | Potassium: 700mg

Spicy Lamb Tenderloin Steaks

Prep. time: 10 min + 30 min marinating **Cook time:** 10 min **Servings:** 4

Ingredients:

- 4 lamb tenderloin steaks (about 4 oz each)
- 2 tbsp olive oil
- 1 tbsp smoked paprika
- 1 tsp ground cumin
- 1/2 tsp cayenne pepper
- 1/2 tsp garlic powder
- 1/2 tsp onion powder
- 1/4 tsp black pepper
- 1/4 tsp salt
- 1 tbsp lemon juice

Directions:

1. Mix olive oil, spices, and lemon juice in a bowl.
2. Coat lamb steaks with mixture and marinate for 30 minutes.
3. Preheat the air fryer to 400°F (200°C).
4. Place lamb steaks in an air fryer basket, ensuring they don't overlap.
5. Cook for 5 minutes, flip, then cook for another 3-5 minutes for medium-rare.
6. Let rest for 5 minutes before serving.

Serving suggestion: Serve with air-fried vegetables or a mixed green salad.

Nutritional Information (per serving): Calories: 220 | Protein: 24g | Carbohydrates: 1g | Fiber: 0.5g | Net Carbs: 0.5g | Fat: 14g | Cholesterol: 70mg | Sodium: 180mg | Potassium: 350mg

Pork

Garlic and Herb Pork Tenderloin

Prep. time: 10 min + 30 min marinating | **Cook time:** 20 min | **Servings:** 4

Ingredients:

- 1 lb pork tenderloin
- 2 tbsp olive oil
- 3 cloves garlic, minced
- 1 tbsp fresh rosemary, chopped
- 1 tbsp fresh thyme leaves
- 1 tsp dried oregano
- 1 tsp Dijon mustard
- 1/2 tsp salt
- 1/4 tsp black pepper

Directions:

1. Mix olive oil, garlic, herbs, mustard, salt, and pepper in a bowl.
2. Coat pork tenderloin with mixture and marinate for 30 minutes.
3. Preheat the air fryer to 400°F (200°C).
4. Place tenderloin in the air fryer basket.
5. Cook for 18-20 minutes, flipping halfway, until internal temperature reaches 145°F (63°C).
6. Let rest for 5 minutes before slicing.

Serving suggestion: Serve with an air-fried vegetable medley or a side salad.

Nutritional Information (per serving): Calories: 200 | Protein: 25g | Carbohydrates: 1g | Fiber: 0.5g | Net Carbs: 0.5g | Fat: 11g | Cholesterol: 75mg | Sodium: 340mg | Potassium: 450mg

Parmesan Crusted Pork Chops

Prep. time: 10 min | **Cook time:** 12 min | **Servings:** 4

Ingredients:

- 4 boneless pork chops (4 oz each)
- 1/2 cup grated Parmesan cheese
- 1/4 cup almond flour
- 1 tsp garlic powder
- 1 tsp dried oregano
- 1/2 tsp paprika
- 1/4 tsp black pepper
- 1 large egg, beaten
- Olive oil spray

Directions:

1. Mix Parmesan, almond flour, garlic powder, oregano, paprika, and pepper in a shallow dish.
2. Dip each pork chop in beaten egg, then coat with Parmesan mixture.
3. Preheat the air fryer to 375°F (190°C).
4. Lightly spray the air fryer basket with olive oil.
5. Place pork chops in a basket without overcrowding.
6. Cook for 10-12 minutes, flipping halfway, until internal temperature reaches 145°F (63°C).

Serving suggestion: Serve with air-fried green beans or a mixed green salad.

Nutritional Information (per serving): Calories: 280 | Protein: 32g | Carbohydrates: 3g | Fiber: 1g | Net Carbs: 2g | Fat: 16g | Cholesterol: 120mg | Sodium: 320mg | Potassium: 450mg

Stuffed Bell Peppers with Ground Pork

Prep. time: 15 min | **Cook time:** 20 min | **Servings:** 4

Ingredients:

- 4 medium bell peppers, any color
- 1 lb lean ground pork
- 1 cup riced cauliflower
- 1/4 cup diced onion
- 2 cloves garlic, minced
- 1 tsp Italian seasoning
- 1/4 cup low-sodium tomato sauce
- 1/4 cup grated Parmesan cheese
- Salt and pepper to taste
- Olive oil spray

Directions:

1. Cut tops off peppers and remove seeds.
2. Cook pork, onion, and garlic in a skillet until pork is browned.
3. Add cauliflower rice, Italian seasoning, tomato sauce, and half the Parmesan. Mix well.
4. Stuff peppers with mixture.
5. Preheat the air fryer to 350°F (175°C).
6. Spray peppers with olive oil and place in an air fryer basket.
7. Cook for 15-20 minutes until peppers are tender.
8. Sprinkle remaining Parmesan on top for the last 2 minutes.

Serving suggestion: Serve with a side salad or air-fried zucchini slices.

Nutritional Information (per serving): Calories: 310 | Protein: 28g | Carbohydrates: 10g | Fiber: 3g | Net Carbs: 7g | Fat: 18g | Cholesterol: 85mg | Sodium: 250mg | Potassium: 550mg

Lean Pork Skewers with Lemon Zest

Prep. time: 10 min + 30 min marinating | **Cook time:** 12 min | **Servings:** 4

Ingredients:

- 1 lb lean pork loin, cut into 1-inch cubes
- 2 tbsp olive oil
- 2 tbsp lemon juice
- 1 tbsp lemon zest
- 2 cloves garlic, minced
- 1 tsp dried oregano
- 1 tsp dried thyme
- 1/2 tsp salt
- 1/4 tsp black pepper
- 1 medium zucchini, cut into 1-inch pieces
- 1 red bell pepper, cut into 1-inch pieces

Directions:

1. Mix olive oil, lemon juice, zest, garlic, herbs, salt, and pepper in a bowl.
2. Add pork cubes, coat well, and marinate for 30 minutes.
3. Preheat the air fryer to 375°F (190°C).
4. Thread pork, zucchini, and bell pepper alternately onto skewers.
5. Place skewers in the air fryer basket, ensuring they don't overlap.
6. Cook for 10-12 minutes, turning halfway, until pork is cooked through.

Serving suggestion: Serve with mixed green salad or air-fried Brussels sprouts.

Nutritional Information (per serving): Calories: 250 | Protein: 28g | Carbohydrates: 6g | Fiber: 2g | Net Carbs: 4g | Fat: 13g | Cholesterol: 75mg | Sodium: 340mg | Potassium: 600mg

Stir-Fried Bok Choy and Shredded Pork

Prep. time: 15 min | **Cook time:** 12 min | **Servings:** 4

Ingredients:

- 12 oz lean pork loin, shredded
- 4 cups Bok choy, chopped
- 2 cloves garlic, minced
- 1 tbsp ginger, grated
- 2 tbsp low-sodium soy sauce
- 1 tbsp rice vinegar
- 1 tsp sesame oil
- 1/4 tsp monk fruit sweetener (optional)
- 1 tbsp olive oil
- 1/4 cup water

Directions:

1. Mix soy sauce, rice vinegar, sesame oil, and sweetener in a small bowl.
2. Preheat the air fryer to 375°F (190°C).
3. Toss pork with half the sauce mixture.
4. Air fry the pork for 6-8 minutes, shaking the basket halfway through.
5. Remove pork, add Bok choy, garlic, ginger, and remaining sauce to the basket.
6. Air fry for 3-4 minutes, stirring halfway.
7. Add pork back, toss everything together, and air fry for 1-2 more minutes.

Serving suggestion: Serve over cauliflower rice or with air-fried shiitake mushrooms.

Nutritional Information (per serving): Calories: 220 | Protein: 25g | Carbohydrates: 5g | Fiber: 2g | Net Carbs: 3g | Fat: 12g | Cholesterol: 65mg | Sodium: 320mg | Potassium: 550mg

Sweet Mustard Glazed Ham Steaks

Prep. time: 10 min | **Cook time:** 10 min | **Servings:** 4

Ingredients:

- 4 ham steaks (4 oz each)
- 2 tbsp Dijon mustard
- 1 tbsp apple cider vinegar
- 1 tbsp olive oil
- 2 tsp erythritol
- 1/4 tsp ground cloves
- 1/4 tsp black pepper

Directions:

1. Mix mustard, vinegar, olive oil, erythritol, cloves, and pepper in a small bowl.
2. Brush both sides of the ham steaks with the mixture.
3. Preheat the air fryer to 375°F (190°C).
4. Place ham steaks in the air fryer basket, not overlapping.
5. Cook for 5 minutes, flip, then cook for another 3-5 minutes until heated through and slightly crispy.

Serving suggestion: Serve with air-fried green beans and mashed cauliflower.

Nutritional Information (per serving): Calories: 200 | Protein: 24g | Carbohydrates: 2g | Fiber: 0g | Net Carbs: 2g | Fat: 11g | Cholesterol: 70mg | Sodium: 980mg | Potassium: 350mg

Chinese-Style Barbecued Pork Ribs

Prep. time: 15 min + 2 hours marinating **Cook time:** 25 min **Servings:** 4

Ingredients:

- 2 lbs pork spare ribs, cut into individual ribs
- 2 tbsp low-sodium soy sauce
- 1 tbsp rice vinegar
- 1 tbsp sesame oil
- 2 tsp five-spice powder
- 2 cloves garlic, minced
- 1 tbsp grated ginger
- 2 tbsp erythritol
- 1 tsp red food coloring (optional, for an authentic look)

Directions:

1. Mix all ingredients except ribs in a bowl to create marinade.
2. Coat ribs with marinade and refrigerate for 2 hours.
3. Preheat the air fryer to 375°F (190°C).
4. Place ribs in an air fryer basket, not overcrowding.
5. Cook for 15 minutes, then flip.
6. Cook for another 10 minutes or until ribs are tender and crispy.

Serving suggestion: Serve with stir-fried Bok choy or air-fried broccoli.

Nutritional Information (per serving): Calories: 380 | Protein: 28g | Carbohydrates: 3g | Fiber: 0g | Net Carbs: 3g | Fat: 29g | Cholesterol: 110mg | Sodium: 320mg | Potassium: 400mg

Rosemary Infused Grilled Boneless Loin Roast

Prep. time: 10 min + 2 hours marinating **Cook time:** 30 min **Servings:** 4

Ingredients:

- 2 lbs boneless pork loin roast
- 2 tbsp olive oil
- 3 cloves garlic, minced
- 2 tbsp fresh rosemary, finely chopped
- 1 tsp lemon zest
- 1 tsp salt
- 1/2 tsp black pepper

Directions:

1. Mix olive oil, garlic, rosemary, lemon zest, salt, and pepper.
2. Rub mixture all over pork loin. Marinate for 2 hours in the refrigerator.
3. Preheat the air fryer to 375°F (190°C).
4. Place pork loin in an air fryer basket.
5. Cook for 25-30 minutes, flipping halfway, until internal temperature reaches 145°F (63°C).
6. Let rest for 5 minutes before slicing.

Serving suggestion: Serve with air-fried asparagus or a mixed green salad.

Nutritional Information (per serving): Calories: 320 | Protein: 40g | Carbohydrates: 1g | Fiber: 0g | Net Carbs: 1g | Fat: 17g | Cholesterol: 120mg | Sodium: 650mg | Potassium: 700mg

Apple Cider Marinated Lean Pulled-Pork Wraps

Prep. time: 15 min + 4 hours marinating **Cook time:** 25 min **Servings:** 4

Ingredients:

- 1 lb pork tenderloin
- 1/4 cup apple cider vinegar
- 1 tbsp olive oil
- 1 tsp Dijon mustard
- 1 tsp erythritol
- 1 tsp smoked paprika
- 1/2 tsp garlic powder
- 1/2 tsp onion powder
- 1/4 tsp salt
- 1/4 tsp black pepper
- 4 large lettuce leaves for wraps
- 1/2 cup shredded red cabbage
- 1/4 cup thinly sliced red onion

Directions:

1. Mix vinegar, oil, mustard, erythritol, and spices for marinade.
2. Marinate pork in refrigerator for 4 hours.
3. Preheat the air fryer to 375°F (190°C).
4. Cook pork for 20-25 minutes, flipping halfway, until internal temperature reaches 145°F (63°C).
5. Rest pork for 5 minutes, then shred with forks.
6. Briefly air fry shredded pork at 400°F (200°C) for 2-3 minutes for crispy edges.
7. Assemble wraps with lettuce, pork, cabbage, and onion.

Serving suggestion: Serve with a side of air-fried zucchini chips.

Nutritional Information (per serving): Calories: 220 | Protein: 28g | Carbohydrates: 5g | Fiber: 2g | Net Carbs: 3g | Fat: 10g | Cholesterol: 75mg | Sodium: 240mg | Potassium: 550mg

Crispy Asian-Inspired Salt & Pepper Spare Ribs

Prep. time: 15 min + 2 hours marinating **Cook time:** 25 min **Servings:** 4

Ingredients:

- 2 lbs pork spare ribs, cut into individual ribs
- 2 tbsp low-sodium soy sauce
- 1 tbsp rice vinegar
- 1 tsp sesame oil
- 2 cloves garlic, minced
- 1 tbsp grated ginger
- 1 tbsp coarse sea salt
- 2 tsp freshly ground black pepper
- 1 tsp Chinese five-spice powder
- 1/4 tsp stevia extract

Directions:

1. Mix soy sauce, vinegar, sesame oil, garlic, ginger, and stevia for marinade.
2. Coat ribs with marinade and refrigerate for 2 hours.
3. Mix salt, pepper, and five-spice powder in a small bowl.
4. Preheat the air fryer to 375°F (190°C).
5. Remove ribs from the marinade and pat dry.
6. Rub ribs with salt and pepper mixture.
7. Air fry ribs for 20-25 minutes, flipping halfway through, until crispy and internal temperature reaches 145°F (63°C).

Serving suggestion: Serve with stir-fried Bok choy or air-fried green beans.

Nutritional Information (per serving): Calories: 390 | Protein: 30g | Carbohydrates: 2g | Fiber: 0g | Net Carbs: 2g | Fat: 29g | Cholesterol: 120mg | Sodium: 780mg | Potassium: 450mg

Spicy Ground Pork Stuffed Mushroom Caps

Prep. time: 15 min | **Cook time:** 12 min | **Servings:** 4

Ingredients:

- 16 large mushroom caps
- 1/2 lb lean ground pork
- 1/4 cup finely chopped onion
- 2 cloves garlic, minced
- 1 small jalapeño, seeded and minced
- 1/4 cup almond flour
- 1 tsp smoked paprika
- 1/2 tsp ground cumin
- 1/4 tsp salt
- 1/4 tsp black pepper
- 2 tbsp grated Parmesan cheese
- 1 tbsp olive oil

Directions:

1. Clean mushrooms and remove stems. Chop stems finely.
2. Mix ground pork, chopped stems, onion, garlic, jalapeño, almond flour, spices, and 1 tbsp Parmesan.
3. Stuff mushroom caps with mixture.
4. Preheat the air fryer to 375°F (190°C).
5. Brush mushrooms with olive oil and place in an air fryer basket.
6. Cook for 10-12 minutes, until pork is cooked and mushrooms are tender.
7. Sprinkle remaining Parmesan on top during the last 2 minutes of cooking.

Serving suggestion: Serve with a side salad of mixed greens.

Nutritional Information (per serving - 4 stuffed mushrooms): Calories: 220 | Protein: 18g | Carbohydrates: 6g | Fiber: 2g | Net Carbs: 4g | Fat: 15g | Cholesterol: 45mg | Sodium: 250mg | Potassium: 450mg

Pork Tenderloin with Fresh Herbs

Prep. time: 10 min + 30 min marinating | **Cook time:** 20 min | **Servings:** 4

Ingredients:

- 1 lb pork tenderloin
- 2 tbsp olive oil
- 2 cloves garlic, minced
- 1 tbsp fresh rosemary, chopped
- 1 tbsp fresh thyme leaves
- 1 tbsp fresh sage, chopped
- 1 tsp lemon zest
- 1/2 tsp salt
- 1/4 tsp black pepper

Directions:

1. Mix olive oil, garlic, herbs, lemon zest, salt, and pepper in a bowl.
2. Coat pork tenderloin with the mixture and marinate for 30 minutes.
3. Preheat the air fryer to 400°F (200°C).
4. Place tenderloin in the air fryer basket.
5. Cook for 18-20 minutes, flipping halfway, until internal temperature reaches 145°F (63°C).
6. Let rest for 5 minutes before slicing.

Serving suggestion: Serve with air-fried asparagus or a mixed green salad.

Nutritional Information (per serving): Calories: 210 | Protein: 26g | Carbohydrates: 1g | Fiber: 0g | Net Carbs: 1g | Fat: 11g | Cholesterol: 75mg | Sodium: 320mg | Potassium: 500mg

Lean Bacon-Wrapped Asparagus Skewers

Prep. time: 15 min | **Cook time:** 10 min | **Servings:** 4

Ingredients:

- 16 asparagus spears, trimmed
- 8 slices lean turkey bacon
- 1 tbsp olive oil
- 1 tsp garlic powder
- 1/4 tsp black pepper
- 1/8 tsp salt
- 1 lemon, cut into wedges

Directions:

1. Preheat the air fryer to 400°F (200°C).
2. Wrap 2 asparagus spears with 1 bacon slice. Repeat for all spears.
3. Brush-wrapped asparagus with olive oil sprinkled with garlic powder, pepper, and salt.
4. Place in the air fryer basket, ensuring no overlap.
5. Cook for 8-10 minutes, turning halfway, until bacon is crispy and asparagus is tender.
6. Thread cooked wraps onto skewers if desired.

Serving suggestion: Serve with lemon wedges for squeezing over the skewers.

Nutritional Information (per serving - 4 bacon-wrapped asparagus spears): Calories: 120 | Protein: 8g | Carbohydrates: 4g | Fiber: 2g | Net Carbs: 2g | Fat: 8g | Cholesterol: 20mg | Sodium: 300mg | Potassium: 230mg

Sweet & Sour Pulled-Pork Lettuce Wraps

Prep. time: 10 min + 4 hours of slow cooking | **Cook time:** 10 min | **Servings:** 4

Ingredients:

- 1 lb pork tenderloin
- 1/4 cup apple cider vinegar
- 2 tbsp tomato paste
- 1 tbsp olive oil
- 2 tsp erythritol
- 1 tsp garlic powder
- 1 tsp onion powder
- 1/2 tsp ground ginger
- 1/4 tsp salt
- 1/4 tsp black pepper
- 8 large lettuce leaves
- 1/2 cup diced cucumber
- 1/4 cup thinly sliced red onion

Directions:

1. Slow-cook pork with vinegar, tomato paste, oil, erythritol, and spices for 4 hours on low.
2. Shred pork and place it in an air fryer basket.
3. Air fry at 380°F (193°C) for 8-10 minutes, stirring halfway, until edges are crispy.
4. Assemble wraps with lettuce, pork, cucumber, and onion.

Serving suggestion: Garnish with sesame seeds and serve with pickled radishes.

Nutritional Information (per serving - 2 lettuce wraps): Calories: 220 | Protein: 28g | Carbohydrates: 6g | Fiber: 2g | Net Carbs: 4g | Fat: 10g | Cholesterol: 75mg | Sodium: 240mg | Potassium: 550mg

Fish and Seafood

Zesty Lemon Garlic Air-Fried Salmon

Prep. time: 10 min **Cook time:** 12 min **Servings:** 4

Ingredients:

- 4 salmon fillets (6 oz each)
- 2 tbsp olive oil
- 2 tbsp lemon juice
- 2 cloves garlic, minced
- 1 tsp lemon zest
- 1 tsp dried dill
- 1/2 tsp salt
- 1/4 tsp black pepper

Directions:

1. Mix olive oil, lemon juice, garlic, lemon zest, dill, salt, and pepper in a bowl.
2. Brush mixture over salmon fillets.
3. Preheat the air fryer to 400°F (200°C).
4. Place salmon in an air fryer basket, skin-side down.
5. Cook for 10-12 minutes, until salmon flakes easily with a fork.

Serving suggestion: Serve with air-fried asparagus or a mixed green salad.

Nutritional Information (per serving): Calories: 320 | Protein: 36g | Carbohydrates: 1g | Fiber: 0g | Net Carbs: 1g | Fat: 19g | Cholesterol: 94mg | Sodium: 340mg | Potassium: 800mg

Shrimp Scampi with Zucchini Noodles

Prep. time: 15 min **Cook time:** 8 min **Servings:** 4

Ingredients:

- 1 lb large shrimp, peeled and deveined
- 4 medium zucchinis, spiralized
- 3 tbsp olive oil
- 4 cloves garlic, minced
- 2 tbsp lemon juice
- 1 tsp lemon zest
- 1/4 cup fresh parsley, chopped
- 1/4 tsp red pepper flakes
- Salt and pepper to taste

Directions:

1. Mix 2 tbsp olive oil, garlic, lemon juice, zest, and red pepper flakes.
2. Toss shrimp in mixture.
3. Preheat air fryer to 380°F (193°C).
4. Air fry shrimp for 5-6 minutes, shaking basket halfway through.
5. In a separate pan, sauté zucchini noodles with 1 tbsp olive oil for 2-3 minutes.
6. Combine shrimp and zoodles and toss with parsley, salt, and pepper.

Serving suggestion: Garnish with lemon wedges and grated Parmesan cheese (if desired).

Nutritional Information (per serving): Calories: 250 | Protein: 25g | Carbohydrates: 8g | Fiber: 2g | Net Carbs: 6g | Fat: 14g | Cholesterol: 170mg | Sodium: 180mg | Potassium: 650mg

Teriyaki Glazed Tuna Steaks

Prep. time: 15 min + 30 min marinating **Cook time:** 8 min **Servings:** 4

Ingredients:

- 4 tuna steaks (6 oz each)
- 1/4 cup low-sodium soy sauce
- 2 tbsp rice vinegar
- 1 tbsp sesame oil
- 2 cloves garlic, minced
- 1 tbsp grated ginger
- 2 tsp erythritol
- 1 tsp xanthan gum (for thickening)
- 1 tbsp sesame seeds
- 2 green onions, sliced (for garnish)

Directions:

1. Mix soy sauce, vinegar, sesame oil, garlic, ginger, and erythritol for marinade.
2. Reserve 1/4 cup marinade; add xanthan gum and set aside.
3. Marinate tuna in the remaining mixture for 30 minutes.
4. Preheat the air fryer to 400°F (200°C).
5. Air fry tuna for 3-4 minutes per side for medium-rare.
6. Brush with reserved glaze and sprinkle with sesame seeds.
7. Air fry for 1 more minute.

Serving suggestion: Serve with air-fried Bok choy or a mixed green salad.

Nutritional Information (per serving): Calories: 280 | Protein: 35g | Carbohydrates: 3g | Fiber: 1g | Net Carbs: 2g | Fat: 14g | Cholesterol: 65mg | Sodium: 400mg | Potassium: 720mg

Chili-Lime Cod Fish Tacos Wrapped in Lettuce

Prep. time: 15 min **Cook time:** 150min **Servings:** 4

Ingredients:

- 1 lb cod fillets
- 2 tbsp olive oil
- 2 tbsp lime juice
- 1 tsp chili powder
- 1 tsp ground cumin
- 1/2 tsp garlic powder
- 1/4 tsp salt
- 8 large lettuce leaves
- 1 cup shredded red cabbage
- 1/2 cup diced tomatoes
- 1/4 cup chopped cilantro
- 1 avocado, sliced

Directions:

1. Mix olive oil, lime juice, chili powder, cumin, garlic powder, and salt.
2. Coat cod fillets with mixture.
3. Preheat the air fryer to 380°F (193°C).
4. Air fry cod for 8-10 minutes, flipping halfway, until flaky.
5. Break cod into chunks.
6. Assemble tacos: lettuce wrap, cod, cabbage, tomatoes, cilantro, and avocado.

Serving suggestion: Serve with lime wedges and a side of cucumber slices.

Nutritional Information (per serving - 2 tacos): Calories: 280 | Protein: 28g | Carbohydrates: 10g | Fiber: 5g | Net Carbs: 5g | Fat: 16g | Cholesterol: 65mg | Sodium: 280mg | Potassium: 850mg

Cajun Spiced Catfish with Sautéed Spinach

Prep. time: 10 min   **Cook time:** 15 min   **Servings:** 4

Ingredients:

- 4 catfish fillets (6 oz each)
- 2 tbsp olive oil
- 1 tbsp Cajun seasoning
- 1/4 tsp salt
- 6 cups fresh spinach
- 2 cloves garlic, minced
- 1 lemon, cut into wedges

Directions:

1. Mix 1 tbsp olive oil with Cajun seasoning and salt. Coat catfish fillets.
2. Preheat the air fryer to 375°F (190°C).
3. Air fry catfish for 10-12 minutes, flipping halfway.
4. Meanwhile, sauté spinach and garlic in 1 tbsp olive oil until wilted.

Serving suggestion: Plate catfish over sautéed spinach. Serve with lemon wedges.

Nutritional Information (per serving): Calories: 270 | Protein: 32g | Carbohydrates: 5g | Fiber: 2g | Net Carbs: 3g | Fat: 15g | Cholesterol: 95mg | Sodium: 350mg | Potassium: 800mg

Herb-Crusted Haddock with Steamed Broccoli

Prep. time: 10 min   **Cook time:** 15 min   **Servings:** 4

Ingredients:

- 4 haddock fillets (6 oz each)
- 1/4 cup almond flour
- 2 tbsp grated Parmesan cheese
- 1 tsp dried thyme
- 1 tsp dried rosemary
- 1/2 tsp garlic powder
- 1/4 tsp salt
- 1/4 tsp black pepper
- 1 egg, beaten
- 4 cups broccoli florets
- 1 lemon, cut into wedges

Directions:

1. Mix almond flour, Parmesan, herbs, garlic powder, salt, and pepper.
2. Dip haddock in egg, then coat with herb mixture.
3. Preheat air fryer to 380°F (193°C).
4. Air fry haddock for 10-12 minutes until crispy and cooked through.
5. Steam broccoli in a separate pot or the microwave.

Serving suggestion: Serve haddock over steamed broccoli with lemon wedges.

Nutritional Information (per serving): Calories: 250 | Protein: 35g | Carbohydrates: 8g | Fiber: 3g | Net Carbs: 5g | Fat: 10g | Cholesterol: 130mg | Sodium: 300mg | Potassium: 700mg

Lemon Pepper Scallops

Prep. time: 10 min | **Cook time:** 8 min | **Servings:** 4

Ingredients:

- 1 lb large sea scallops (about 16)
- 2 tbsp olive oil
- 2 tsp lemon zest
- 2 tbsp lemon juice
- 1 tsp freshly ground black pepper
- 1/4 tsp salt
- 1 clove garlic, minced
- 4 cups mixed salad greens
- 1 lemon, cut into wedges

Directions:

1. Pat scallops dry with paper towels.
2. Mix olive oil, lemon zest, lemon juice, pepper, salt, and garlic.
3. Coat scallops with mixture.
4. Preheat the air fryer to 400°F (200°C).
5. Place scallops in the air fryer basket, not touching.
6. Cook for 3-4 minutes, flip, then cook 2-3 minutes more until golden.

Serving suggestion: Serve scallops over mixed greens with lemon wedges.

Nutritional Information (per serving): Calories: 180 | Protein: 20g | Carbohydrates: 5g | Fiber: 1g | Net Carbs: 4g | Fat: 9g | Cholesterol: 35mg | Sodium: 300mg | Potassium: 400mg

Cajun Shrimp Skewers with Grilled Bell Peppers

Prep. time: 15 min + 30 min marinating | **Cook time:** 10 min | **Servings:** 4

Ingredients:

- 1 lb large shrimp, peeled and deveined
- 2 bell peppers, mixed colors, cut into chunks
- 2 tbsp olive oil
- 2 tsp Cajun seasoning
- 1 tsp paprika
- 1/2 tsp garlic powder
- 1/4 tsp cayenne pepper
- 1/4 tsp salt
- 1 lemon, cut into wedges

Directions:

1. Mix olive oil, Cajun seasoning, paprika, garlic powder, cayenne, and salt.
2. Toss shrimp and bell peppers in the mixture. Marinate for 30 minutes.
3. Preheat air fryer to 380°F (193°C).
4. Thread shrimp and peppers onto skewers.
5. Air fry for 5 minutes, flip skewers, then cook for 3-5 more minutes until shrimp are pink and peppers are tender-crisp.

Serving suggestion: Serve with lemon wedges and a side salad of mixed greens.

Nutritional Information (per serving): Calories: 190 | Protein: 24g | Carbohydrates: 6g | Fiber: 2g | Net Carbs: 4g | Fat: 9g | Cholesterol: 170mg | Sodium: 380mg | Potassium: 350mg

Asian-Style Sesame Ginger Salmon Patties

Prep. time: 15 min   **Cook time:** 10 min   **Servings:** 4

Ingredients:

- 1 lb canned salmon, drained and flaked
- 1/4 cup almond flour
- 2 green onions, finely chopped
- 1 egg
- 1 tbsp sesame oil
- 1 tbsp grated fresh ginger
- 1 clove garlic, minced
- 1 tbsp low-sodium soy sauce
- 1 tsp erythritol
- 1 tbsp sesame seeds
- Olive oil spray

Directions:

1. Mix all ingredients except olive oil spray in a bowl.
2. Form the mixture into 8 patties.
3. Preheat the air fryer to 375°F (190°C).
4. Lightly spray the air fryer basket with olive oil.
5. Place patties in the basket, not overcrowding.
6. Cook for 5 minutes, flip, then cook for 4-5 more minutes until golden and crispy.

Serving suggestion: Serve with a side of cucumber salad or steamed Bok choy.

Nutritional Information (per serving - 2 patties): Calories: 280 | Protein: 28g | Carbohydrates: 4g | Fiber: 2g | Net Carbs: 2g | Fat: 17g | Cholesterol: 110mg | Sodium: 350mg | Potassium: 450mg

Mediterranean Stuffed Calamari Rings

Prep. time: 20 min   **Cook time:** 10 min   **Servings:** 4

Ingredients:

- 1 lb cleaned calamari rings
- 1/2 cup almond flour
- 1/4 cup finely chopped sun-dried tomatoes
- 1/4 cup crumbled feta cheese
- 2 tbsp chopped fresh basil
- 2 cloves garlic, minced
- 1 tbsp olive oil
- 1 tsp dried oregano
- 1/4 tsp red pepper flakes
- Salt and pepper to taste
- Lemon wedges for serving

Directions:

1. Mix almond flour, sun-dried tomatoes, feta, basil, garlic, olive oil, oregano, and red pepper flakes.
2. Stuff calamari rings with mixture.
3. Preheat air fryer to 380°F (193°C).
4. Place stuffed calamari in an air fryer basket without overcrowding.
5. Cook for 5 minutes, gently turn, then cook for 3-5 more minutes until golden and crispy.

Serving suggestion: Serve with lemon wedges and a side of mixed greens.

Nutritional Information (per serving): Calories: 260 | Protein: 24g | Carbohydrates: 8g | Fiber: 3g | Net Carbs: 5g | Fat: 16g | Cholesterol: 260mg | Sodium: 320mg | Potassium: 380mg

Spicy Panko Crusted Tilapia Filets

Prep. time: 15 min **Cook time:** 10 min **Servings:** 4

Ingredients:

- 4 tilapia fillets (6 oz each)
- 1/2 cup almond flour
- 1/4 cup panko breadcrumbs
- 1 tsp paprika
- 1/2 tsp cayenne pepper
- 1/2 tsp garlic powder
- 1/4 tsp salt
- 1 egg, beaten
- Olive oil spray
- Lemon wedges for serving

Directions:

1. Mix almond flour, panko, paprika, cayenne, garlic powder, and salt in a shallow dish.
2. Dip each tilapia fillet in a beaten egg, then coat it with the panko mixture.
3. Preheat the air fryer to 400°F (200°C).
4. Lightly spray the air fryer basket with olive oil.
5. Place coated fillets in the basket, not overcrowding.
6. Spray the tops of the fillets lightly with olive oil.
7. Cook for 5 minutes, flip, then cook for 4-5 more minutes until golden and crispy.

Serving suggestion: Serve with lemon wedges and steamed broccoli or mixed green salad.

Nutritional Information (per serving): Calories: 290 | Protein: 35g | Carbohydrates: 8g | Fiber: 2g | Net Carbs: 6g | Fat: 13g | Cholesterol: 110mg | Sodium: 260mg | Potassium: 480mg

Fragrant Halibut Steaks with Citrus Vinaigrette

Prep. time: 15 min **Cook time:** 10 min **Servings:** 4

Ingredients:

- 4 halibut steaks (6 oz each)
- 2 tbsp olive oil
- 1 tsp dried thyme
- 1 tsp dried rosemary
- 1/2 tsp garlic powder
- 1/4 tsp salt
- 1/4 tsp black pepper

For the vinaigrette:

- 2 tbsp lemon juice
- 1 tbsp orange juice
- 1 tbsp olive oil
- 1 tsp Dijon mustard
- 1 tsp erythritol
- 1 clove garlic, minced

Directions:

1. Mix olive oil, thyme, rosemary, garlic powder, salt, and pepper. Coat halibut steaks.
2. Preheat air fryer to 380°F (193°C).
3. Place halibut in an air fryer basket, not overcrowding.
4. Cook for 8-10 minutes, flipping halfway, until fish flakes easily.
5. Meanwhile, whisk all vinaigrette ingredients together.

Serving suggestion: Drizzle vinaigrette over cooked halibut. Serve with air-fried asparagus or a mixed green salad.

Nutritional Information (per serving): Calories: 290 | Protein: 35g | Carbohydrates: 2g | Fiber: 0g | Net Carbs: 2g | Fat: 16g | Cholesterol: 85mg | Sodium: 250mg | Potassium: 700mg

Mushroom Caps Stuffed with Clams

Prep. time: 20 min **Cook time:** 12 min **Servings:** 4

Ingredients:

- 16 large mushroom caps
- 6 oz canned clams, drained and chopped
- 2 slices bacon, cooked and crumbled
- 1/4 cup almond flour
- 2 tbsp grated Parmesan cheese
- 2 tbsp finely chopped red bell pepper
- 1 clove garlic, minced
- 1 tbsp chopped fresh parsley
- 1 tsp lemon juice
- 1/4 tsp red pepper flakes
- Salt and pepper to taste
- Olive oil spray

Directions:

1. Clean mushrooms and remove stems. Chop stems finely.
2. Mix chopped stems, clams, bacon, almond flour, Parmesan, bell pepper, garlic, parsley, lemon juice, red pepper flakes, salt, and pepper.
3. Stuff the mixture into mushroom caps.
4. Preheat the air fryer to 375°F (190°C).
5. Lightly spray the air fryer basket with olive oil.
6. Place stuffed mushrooms in the basket, not overcrowding.
7. Cook for 10-12 minutes until mushrooms are tender and tops are golden.

Serving suggestion: Serve as an appetizer or with a side salad for a light meal.

Nutritional Information (per serving - 4 stuffed mushrooms): Calories: 140 | Protein: 12g | Carbohydrates: 6g | Fiber: 2g | Net Carbs: 4g | Fat: 8g | Cholesterol: 25mg | Sodium: 250mg | Potassium: 300mg

Coconut Shrimp with Avocado Dip

Prep. time: 15 min **Cook time:** 18 min **Servings:** 4

Ingredients:

For the shrimp:
- 1 lb large shrimp, peeled and deveined
- 1/2 cup almond flour
- 1/2 cup unsweetened shredded coconut
- 1 tsp garlic powder
- 1/2 tsp paprika
- 1/4 tsp salt
- 2 eggs, beaten
- Olive oil spray

For the avocado dip:
- 1 ripe avocado
- 2 tbsp lime juice
- 1 tbsp cilantro, chopped
- Salt to taste

Directions:

1. Mix almond flour, coconut, garlic powder, paprika, and salt in a shallow dish.
2. Dip each shrimp in a beaten egg, then coat it with coconut.
3. Preheat air fryer to 380°F (193°C).
4. Place coated shrimp in an air fryer basket, not overcrowding. Spray lightly with olive oil.
5. Cook for 4 minutes, flip, then cook for 3-4 more minutes until golden and crispy.
6. For the dip, mash avocado with lime juice, cilantro, and salt.

Serving suggestion: Serve shrimp with avocado dip and lemon wedges.

Nutritional Information (per serving): Calories: 320 | Protein: 25g | Carbohydrates: 10g | Fiber: 6g | Net Carbs: 4g | Fat: 22g | Cholesterol: 210mg | Sodium: 380mg | Potassium: 450mg

Desserts

Cinnamon and Almond Biscotti

Prep. time: 15 min **Cook time:** 25 min **Servings:** 16 biscotti (4 servings, 4 biscotti each)

Ingredients:

- 2 cups almond flour
- 1/4 cup erythritol
- 1 tsp baking powder
- 2 tsp ground cinnamon
- 1/4 tsp salt
- 2 large eggs
- 2 tbsp melted coconut oil
- 1 tsp vanilla extract
- 1/2 cup sliced almonds

Directions:

1. Mix almond flour, erythritol, baking powder, cinnamon, and salt.
2. Whisk eggs, coconut oil, and vanilla in another bowl.
3. Combine wet and dry ingredients. Fold in almonds.
4. Form dough into a log (8" x 4").
5. Preheat the air fryer to 300°F (150°C).
6. Air fry for 20 minutes until golden.
7. Let cool for 10 minutes, then slice into 16 pieces.
8. Air fry slices at 300°F for 5 minutes, flip and cook for 3-5 more until crisp.

Serving suggestion: Enjoy with a cup of sugar-free coffee or tea.

Nutritional Information (per serving - 4 biscotti): Calories: 340 | Protein: 12g | Carbohydrates: 10g | Fiber: 6g | Net Carbs: 4g | Fat: 30g | Cholesterol: 90mg | Sodium: 180mg | Potassium: 240mg

Coconut and Blueberry Cheesecake Bites

Prep. time: 20 min **Cook time:** 10 min **Servings:** 12 bites (3 per serving)

Ingredients:

For the crust:

- 1 cup almond flour
- 2 tbsp unsweetened shredded coconut
- 2 tbsp melted coconut oil
- 1 tbsp erythritol

For the filling:

- 8 oz cream cheese, softened
- 1/4 cup erythritol
- 1 large egg
- 1 tsp vanilla extract
- 1/4 cup fresh blueberries

Directions:

1. Mix crust ingredients. Press into 12 silicone muffin cups.
2. Preheat the air fryer to 300°F (150°C).
3. Beat cream cheese, erythritol, egg, and vanilla until smooth.
4. Pour filling over crusts. Top each with 2-3 blueberries.
5. Air fry for 8-10 minutes until set but slightly jiggly.
6. Cool completely, then refrigerate for 2 hours.

Serving suggestion: Garnish with a sprinkle of unsweetened coconut flakes.

Nutritional Information (per serving - 3 bites): Calories: 380 | Protein: 10g | Carbohydrates: 8g | Fiber: 3g | Net Carbs: 5g | Fat: 35g | Cholesterol: 105mg | Sodium: 230mg | Potassium: 160mg

Dark Chocolate Dipped Strawberries

Prep. time: 10 min **Cook time:** 5 min **Servings:** 4 (4 strawberries each)

Ingredients:

- 16 large fresh strawberries, washed and dried
- 4 oz 85% dark chocolate, chopped
- 1 tbsp coconut oil
- 1 tbsp powdered erythritol (optional for dusting)

Directions:

1. Melt chocolate and coconut oil in a microwave-safe bowl in 30-second intervals, stirring until smooth.
2. Dip each strawberry halfway into the chocolate mixture.
3. Place dipped strawberries on a parchment-lined air fryer basket.
4. Air fry at 300°F (150°C) for 2 minutes.
5. Remove and let cool for 1 minute.
6. Air fry again at 300°F for 1 minute.
7. Dust with powdered erythritol if desired.
8. Refrigerate for 15 minutes before serving.

Serving suggestion: Serve chilled as a light dessert or snack.

Nutritional Information (per serving - 4 strawberries): Calories: 120 | Protein: 2g | Carbohydrates: 10g | Fiber: 4g | Net Carbs: 6g | Fat: 9g | Cholesterol: 0mg | Sodium: 1mg | Potassium: 170mg

Vanilla Bean Custard Stuffed Peaches

Prep. time: 15 min **Cook time:** 15 min **Servings:** 4

Ingredients:

- 4 medium ripe peaches, halved and pitted
- 1 cup unsweetened almond milk
- 2 large eggs
- 2 tbsp erythritol
- 1 tsp vanilla bean paste
- 1/4 tsp xanthan gum
- Pinch of salt
- 1/4 tsp ground cinnamon

Directions:

1. Blend almond milk, eggs, erythritol, vanilla bean paste, xanthan gum, and salt until smooth.
2. Pour the mixture into a heat-safe dish that fits in your air fryer.
3. Air fry at 300°F (150°C) for 10-12 minutes, stirring every 3 minutes, until custard thickens.
4. Chill custard for 1 hour.
5. Preheat the air fryer to 350°F (175°C).
6. Place peach halves in the air fryer basket and cut side up.
7. Air fry for 5-7 minutes until softened.
8. Fill peach halves with chilled custard and sprinkle with cinnamon.

Serving suggestion: Serve immediately as a light dessert.

Nutritional Information (per serving - 2 peach halves with custard): Calories: 120 | Protein: 5g | Carbohydrates: 15g | Fiber: 3g | Net Carbs: 12g | Fat: 5g | Cholesterol: 95mg | Sodium: 70mg | Potassium: 250mg

Almond Joy Keto Cookies

Prep. time: 15 min **Cook time:** 10 min **Servings:** 12 cookies (3 per serving)

Ingredients:

- 1 1/2 cups almond flour
- 1/4 cup unsweetened shredded coconut
- 1/4 cup erythritol
- 1/4 cup sugar-free dark chocolate chips
- 1/4 cup sliced almonds
- 1 large egg
- 3 tbsp coconut oil, melted
- 1 tsp vanilla extract
- 1/4 tsp salt

Directions:

1. Mix almond flour, coconut, erythritol, and salt in a bowl.
2. Whisk egg, melted coconut oil, and vanilla in another bowl.
3. Combine wet and dry ingredients. Fold in chocolate chips and almonds.
4. Form 12 cookies and place them on parchment paper in an air fryer basket.
5. Air fry at 320°F (160°C) for 8-10 minutes, until golden brown.
6. Let cool completely before serving.

Serving suggestion: Enjoy with a glass of unsweetened almond milk.

Nutritional Information (per serving - 3 cookies): Calories: 320 | Protein: 9g | Carbohydrates: 8g | Fiber: 5g | Net Carbs: 3g | Fat: 29g | Cholesterol: 45mg | Sodium: 150mg | Potassium: 180mg

Peanut Butter Banana Muffins

Prep. time: 10 min **Cook time:** 15 min **Servings:** 4

Ingredients:

- 1 cup almond flour
- 1/4 cup coconut flour
- 2 tbsp erythritol
- 1 tsp baking powder
- 1/4 tsp salt
- 2 ripe bananas, mashed
- 1/4 cup natural peanut butter
- 2 large eggs
- 1 tsp vanilla extract
- 1/4 cup unsweetened almond milk

Directions:

1. Mix dry ingredients in a bowl: almond flour, coconut flour, erythritol, baking powder, and salt.
2. Whisk mashed bananas, peanut butter, eggs, vanilla, and almond milk in another bowl.
3. Combine wet and dry ingredients until well-mixed.
4. Line the air fryer basket with parchment paper.
5. Scoop batter into 8 silicone muffin cups.
6. Place muffin cups in the air fryer basket.
7. Air fry at 320°F (160°C) for 12 minutes until a toothpick comes out clean.
8. Let cool before serving.

Serving suggestion: Enjoy warm or at room temperature.

Nutritional Information (per serving - 2 muffins): Calories: 310 | Protein: 12g | Carbohydrates: 20g | Fiber: 7g | Net Carbs: 13g | Fat: 23g | Cholesterol: 90mg | Sodium: 220mg | Potassium: 300mg

Lemon Blueberry Cake

Prep. time: 15 min **Cook time:** 25 min **Servings:** 4

Ingredients:

- 1 1/2 cups almond flour
- 1/4 cup coconut flour
- 1/3 cup erythritol
- 2 tsp baking powder
- 1/4 tsp salt
- 3 large eggs
- 1/4 cup unsweetened almond milk
- 1/4 cup melted coconut oil
- 2 tbsp lemon juice
- 1 tbsp lemon zest
- 1 tsp vanilla extract
- 1/2 cup fresh blueberries

Directions:

1. Mix dry ingredients in a bowl: almond flour, coconut flour, erythritol, baking powder, and salt.
2. Whisk eggs, almond milk, coconut oil, lemon juice, lemon zest, and vanilla in another bowl.
3. Combine wet and dry ingredients until smooth.
4. Gently fold in blueberries.
5. Line a 6-inch cake pan with parchment paper and pour in batter.
6. Place pan in air fryer basket.
7. Air fry at 300°F (150°C) for 25 minutes or until a toothpick comes out clean.
8. Let cool before serving.

Serving suggestion: Garnish with a few fresh blueberries and a sprinkle of powdered erythritol if desired.

Nutritional Information (per serving): | Calories: 340 | Protein: 12g | Carbohydrates: 15g | Fiber: 7g | Net Carbs: 8g | Fat: 28g | Cholesterol: 140mg | Sodium: 270mg | Potassium: 200mg

Cinnamon Apple Chips with a Touch of Stevia

Prep. time: 10 min **Cook time:** 2 hours **Servings:** 4

Ingredients:

- 2 large Granny Smith apples
- 1 tsp ground cinnamon
- 1/8 tsp pure stevia powder
- 1/8 tsp salt

Directions:

1. Wash and core apples. Slice very thinly (1/8 inch) using a mandoline or sharp knife.
2. Mix cinnamon, stevia, and salt in a small bowl.
3. Arrange apple slices in a single layer in the air fryer basket.
4. Sprinkle half the cinnamon mixture over the slices.
5. Air fry at 300°F (150°C) for 15 minutes.
6. Flip slices and sprinkle with the remaining cinnamon mixture.
7. Continue air frying at 250°F (120°C) for 30-45 minutes, checking every 5 minutes and removing crisp chips as they're done.
8. Repeat the process with the remaining apple slices.

Serving suggestion: Enjoy as a snack or crumble over Greek yogurt for added crunch.

Nutritional Information (per serving): Calories: 45 | Protein: 0.2g | Carbohydrates: 12g | Fiber: 2g | Net Carbs: 10g | Fat: 0.1g | Cholesterol: 0mg | Sodium: 75mg | Potassium: 100mg

Gluten-Free Strawberry Rhubarb Crumble

Prep. time: 15 min **Cook time:** 20 min **Servings:** 4

Ingredients:

For the filling:
- 1 cup strawberries, hulled and quartered
- 1 cup rhubarb, chopped
- 2 tbsp erythritol
- 1 tsp lemon juice

For the crumble:
- 1/2 cup almond flour
- 1/4 cup chopped walnuts
- 2 tbsp coconut flour
- 2 tbsp erythritol
- 1/4 tsp cinnamon
- 2 tbsp coconut oil,

Directions:

1. Mix the filling ingredients in a bowl.
2. In another bowl, combine crumble ingredients.
3. Divide filling among 4 ramekins or a small baking dish that fits in your air fryer.
4. Top with crumble mixture.
5. Place in air fryer basket.
6. Air fry at 320°F (160°C) for 15-20 minutes, until fruit is bubbly and topping is golden.

Serving suggestion: Serve warm, optionally topped with a dollop of Greek yogurt.

Nutritional Information (per serving): Calories: 220 | Protein: 5g | Carbohydrates: 14g | Fiber: 5g | Net Carbs: 9g | Fat: 18g | Cholesterol: 0mg | Sodium: 5mg | Potassium: 180mg

Chia Raspberry Jam Filled Doughnut Holes

Prep. time: 10 min **Cook time:** 15 min **Servings:** 16 doughnut holes (4 per serving)

Ingredients:

For the doughnut holes:
- 1 cup almond flour
- 1/4 cup coconut flour
- 1/4 cup erythritol
- 1 tsp baking powder
- 1/4 tsp salt
- 2 large eggs
- 1/4 cup unsweetened almond milk
- 2 tbsp coconut oil, melted
- 1 tsp vanilla extract

For the chia raspberry jam:
- 1/2 cup fresh raspberries
- 1 tbsp chia seeds
- 1 tbsp erythritol

Directions:

1. Make jam: Mash raspberries with erythritol and stir in chia seeds. Let sit for 15 minutes.
2. Mix dry ingredients for doughnut holes in a bowl.
3. Whisk eggs, almond milk, coconut oil, and vanilla in another bowl.
4. Combine wet and dry ingredients to form a dough.
5. Form 16 small balls, make a depression in each, and fill with 1/2 tsp jam. Seal the holes.
6. Preheat the air fryer to 350°F (175°C).
7. Place doughnut holes in the basket, not touching.
8. Air fry for 8-10 minutes, shaking basket halfway through, until golden.

Serving suggestion: Dust with powdered erythritol if desired.

Nutritional Information (per serving - 4 doughnut holes): Calories: 280 | Protein: 10g | Carbohydrates: 14g | Fiber: 7g | Net Carbs: 7g | Fat: 22g | Cholesterol: 95mg | Sodium: 220mg | Potassium: 180mg

Low-Sugar Hazelnut Chocolate Truffles

Prep. time: 20 min | **Cook time:** 5 min | **Servings:** 12 truffles (3 per serving)

Ingredients:

- 1 cup hazelnuts
- 4 oz unsweetened dark chocolate (90% cocoa or higher)
- 1/4 cup heavy cream
- 2 tbsp erythritol
- 1 tsp vanilla extract
- 1/8 tsp salt
- 2 tbsp unsweetened cocoa powder

Directions:

1. Air fry hazelnuts at 320°F (160°C) for 5 minutes, shaking halfway. Cool and chop finely.
2. Melt chocolate in a microwave-safe bowl.
3. Heat cream until steaming; pour over chocolate. Add erythritol, vanilla, and salt. Stir until smooth.
4. Mix in chopped hazelnuts. Chill mixture for 1 hour.
5. Form into 12 balls. Roll in cocoa powder.
6. Chill until firm.

Serving suggestion: Serve chilled as a dessert or with coffee.

Nutritional Information (per serving - 3 truffles): Calories: 240 | Protein: 5g | Carbohydrates: 10g | Fiber: 5g | Net Carbs: 5g | Fat: 22g | Cholesterol: 15mg | Sodium: 40mg | Potassium: 220mg

Berries and Oats Crunchy Granola Bars

Prep. time: 15 min | **Cook time:** 15 min | **Servings:** 8 bars (2 per serving)

Ingredients:

- 1 cup rolled oats
- 1/2 cup chopped almonds
- 1/4 cup ground flaxseed
- 1/4 cup unsweetened shredded coconut
- 1/4 cup freeze-dried mixed berries
- 2 tbsp erythritol
- 1/4 tsp cinnamon
- 1/4 cup almond butter
- 2 tbsp coconut oil, melted
- 1 tsp vanilla extract

Directions:

1. Mix dry ingredients in a bowl: oats, almonds, flaxseed, coconut, berries, erythritol, and cinnamon.
2. Whisk almond butter, coconut oil, and vanilla in another bowl.
3. Combine wet and dry ingredients.
4. Line the air fryer basket with parchment paper.
5. Press the mixture firmly into the basket, about 1/2 inch thick.
6. Air fry at 300°F (150°C) for 15 minutes, checking every 5 minutes to prevent burning.
7. Let cool completely before cutting into 8 bars.

Serving suggestion: Enjoy as a snack or crumbled over Greek yogurt.

Nutritional Information (per serving - 2 bars): Calories: 280 | Protein: 8g | Carbohydrates: 18g | Fiber: 7g | Net Carbs: 11g | Fat: 22g | Cholesterol: 0mg | Sodium: 5mg | Potassium: 220mg

Keto Avocado Brownies

Prep. time: 15 min **Cook time:** 20 min **Servings:** 8 brownies (2 per serving)

Ingredients:

- 1 ripe avocado, mashed
- 2 large eggs
- 1/4 cup erythritol
- 1/4 cup unsweetened cocoa powder
- 1/2 cup almond flour
- 1/4 tsp baking soda
- 1/4 tsp salt
- 1/4 cup sugar-free dark chocolate chips
- 1 tsp vanilla extract

Directions:

1. Blend avocado, eggs, erythritol, and vanilla until smooth.
2. Mix cocoa powder, almond flour, baking soda, and salt.
3. Fold in chocolate chips.
4. Line the air fryer basket with parchment paper.
5. Pour batter into the basket, spreading evenly.
6. Air fry at 300°F (150°C) for 20 minutes or until a toothpick comes out clean.
7. Let cool before cutting into 8 squares.

Serving suggestion: Enjoy with a dollop of sugar-free whipped cream or a few berries.

Nutritional Information (per serving - 2 brownies): Calories: 220 | Protein: 8g | Carbohydrates: 10g | Fiber: 6g | Net Carbs: 4g | Fat: 18g | Cholesterol: 95mg | Sodium: 220mg | Potassium: 300mg

Creamy Greek Yogurt Cheesecake with Mixed Berries

Prep. time: 15 min **Cook time:** 25 min **Servings:** 4

Ingredients:

For the crust:
- 1 cup almond flour
- 2 tbsp melted coconut oil
- 1 tbsp erythritol

For the filling:
- 1 cup full-fat Greek yogurt
- 8 oz cream cheese, softened
- 1/4 cup erythritol
- 2 large eggs
- 1 tsp vanilla extract
- 1 tbsp lemon juice

For topping:
- 1/2 cup mixed berries

Directions:

1. Mix crust ingredients and press into a 6-inch springform pan.
2. Beat the filling ingredients until smooth. Pour over the crust.
3. Preheat the air fryer to 300°F (150°C).
4. Place pan in air fryer basket. Cook for 25 minutes or until the center is almost set.
5. Let cool, then refrigerate for 2 hours.
6. Top with mixed berries before serving.

Serving suggestion: Garnish with a mint leaf for added freshness.

Nutritional Information (per serving): Calories: 380 | Protein: 15g | Carbohydrates: 12g | Fiber: 3g | Net Carbs: 9g | Fat: 32g | Cholesterol: 145mg | Sodium: 220mg | Potassium: 180mg

30-day Meal Plan

	Breakfast	**Lunch**	**Dinner**	**Dessert**
Day 1	Vegetable & Egg Muffins p. 12	Greek Yogurt Marinated Chicken Skewers and Stuffed Mushroom Caps with Spinach and Ricotta p.75, 46	Low-Carb Caesar Salad with Air-Fried Shrimp p. 29	Berries and Oats Crunchy Granola Bars p. 113
Day 2	Breakfast Pizza on Cauliflower Crust p. 22	Asian-Style Sesame Ginger Salmon Patties and Garlic-Parmesan Air Fryer Brussels Sprouts p. 104, 46	Grilled Chicken and Avocado Salad p. 33	Vanilla Bean Custard Stuffed Peaches p. 109
Day 3	Coconut Flour Pumpkin Pancakes p.16	Shepherd's Pie with Cauliflower Mash and Sweet & Savory Butternut Squash Wedges p. 85, 44	Buffalo Chicken Wings with Celery Sticks p. 67	Dark Chocolate Dipped Strawberries p. 109
Day 4	Stuffed Bell Peppers with Eggs and Turkey Sausage p. 17	Curry-Spiced Chicken Thighs and Fresh Garden Vegetable Quinoa Bowl p. 75, 31	Marinated Artichoke Heart and Shrimp Pasta-Salad p. 31	Almond Joy Keto Cookies p. 110
Day 5	Almond Flour Cinnamon Muffins p. 14	Parmesan-Crusted Turkey Tenders with Warm Mushroom and Spinach Salad p. 62, 36	Beef and Broccoli Stir-fry p.77	Peanut Butter Banana Muffins p. 110
Day 6	Low-sugar Apple Fritters p. 18	Zesty Lemon Garlic Air-Fried Salmon Fillets with Cauliflower Rice Pilaf with Carrots and Peas p. 100, 42	Spicy Chicken & Veggie Soup with Tortilla Strips p. 49	Coconut and Blueberry Cheesecake Bites p. 108
Day 7	Cauliflower Hash Browns p. 20	Crispy Turkey Tacos with Avocado Crema and Italian Herb Roasted Bell Peppers p.56, 43	Vegetable Barley Soup p. 49	Chia Raspberry Jam Filled Doughnut Holes p. 112

Day 8	Cinnamon-Spiced Zucchini Bread Slices p. 12	Lemon-infused Chicken Breast with Steamed Broccoli and Warm Mediterranean Vegetable Salad p.66, 35	Warm Halloumi and Tomato Salad p. 37	Cinnamon Apple Chips with a Touch of Stevia p. 111
Day 9	Chickpea Pancakes with Herbs p.18	Healthy Chicken Cordon Bleu with Warm Mediterranean Vegetable Salad p. 67, 35	Teriyaki Glazed Tuna Steaks p. 101	Creamy Greek Yogurt Cheesecake with Mixed Berries p. 114
Day 10	Vegetable and Cheese Frittata p.20	Hearty Grilled Aubergine & Ground Beef Lasagna with Garlic & Rosemary Roasted Turnips p.82, 42	Chicken Meatball Italian Wedding Soup p. 53	Lemon Blueberry Cake p. 111
Day 11	Smoked Salmon and Avocado Toast p.13	Hearty Turkey and Bean Chili Soup and Parmesan Zucchini Fries p. 52	Mediterranean Stuffed Calamari Rings with Spicy Okra with Cool Yogurt Dip p.104, 41	Berries and Oats Crunchy Granola Bars p. 113
Day 12	Egg and Cheese Stuffed Tomatoes p.23	Spicy Buffalo Chicken Wings with Celery Sticks and Summer Berry Almond Spinach Salad p.67, 32	Spinach & Minced lamb stuffed Zucchini boats p. 89	Vanilla Bean Custard Stuffed Peaches p.109
Day 13	Breakfast Sweet Potato Boats p.25	Greek-Style Turkey Burgers with Tzatziki p. 64	Chicken Zoodle Pro p. 52	Low-Sugar Hazelnut Chocolate Truffles p. 113
Day 14	Asparagus and Mushroom Scramble p.17	Cauliflower & Cheddar Cheese Soup and Warm Salmon Niçoise Salad p.50, 33	Turkey Zucchini Boats with Mozzarella Topping p. 60	Keto Avocado Brownies p.114
Day 15	Protein-Packed Quinoa Breakfast Bowl p.15	Asian Inspired Sesame-Ginger Ground Turkey Wraps and Crispy Air-Fried Chickpea Salad p. 61, 35	Grilled Salmon Kale Salad with Lemon Dressing p. 30	Cinnamon Apple Chips with a Touch of Stevia p. 111

Day	Breakfast	Lunch	Dinner	Dessert/Snack
Day 16	Breakfast Burrito Bowl p.24	Greek Style Stuffed Bell Peppers with Ground Lamb and Lemon-Pepper Asparagus Spears p.86, 39	Chicken Piccata with Capers p. 72	Gluten-Free Strawberry Rhubarb Crumble p. 112
Day 17	Cheesy Spinach Air Fryer Omelette p.13	Coconut Shrimp with Avocado Dip with Lemon-Pepper Asparagus Spears p. 106, 39	Marinated Artichoke Heart and Shrimp Pasta-Salad p. 31	Lemon Blueberry Cake p. 111
Day 18	Southwest Black Bean and Sweet Potato Breakfast Bowl p. 16	Turkey Zucchini Boats with Mozzarella Topping and Beetroot and Feta Salad p.60, 37	Mushroom Caps Stuffed with Clams p. 106	Almond Joy Keto Cookies p. 110
Day 19	Avocado Egg Boats p.14	Homemade Beef Meatballs with Spicy Sweet Potato and Black Bean Salad p.80, 34	Hearty Turkey and Bean Chili Soup p. 52	Sugar-Free Cinnamon and Almond Biscotti p.108
Day 20	Blueberry Lemon Scones p.25	Rosemary & Garlic Infused Turkey Legs and Spinach & Strawberry Salad with Balsamic Vinaigrette p. 58, 29	Cauliflower 'Mac' and Cheese p. 40	Dark Chocolate Dipped Strawberries p. 109
Day 21	Low-Carb Breakfast Burritos p. 15	Stuffed Bell Peppers with Ground Beef and Air-Fried Green Beans Almondine p. 77, 39	Teriyaki Turkey Skewers with Pineapple p. 64	Coconut and Blueberry Cheesecake Bites p. 108
Day 22	Chickpea Avocado Toast p. 19	Savory Garlic & Herb Chicken Drumsticks with Pear and Walnut Winter Salad p.66, 36	Herb-Crusted Haddock with Steamed Broccoli p. 102	Berries and Oats Crunchy Granola Bars p. 113
Day 23	Zucchini and Carrot Morning Glory Muffins p. 24	Spicy Ground Turkey Lettuce Wraps with Crispy Brussels Sprouts with Balsamic Glaze p. 57, 41	Spicy Ground Beef Lettuce Wraps with Avocado Salsa p. 79	Peanut Butter Banana Muffins p. 110

Day 24	Berry Chia Seed Breakfast Bars p. 19	Spicy Ground Pork Stuffed Mushroom Caps with Warm Halloumi and Tomato Salad p. 97, 37	Grilled Chicken and Avocado Salad p. 33	Vanilla Bean Custard Stuffed Peaches p. 109
Day 25	Almond Flour Banana Bread Slices p. 21	Chicken and Zucchini Meatballs with Cauliflower 'Mac' and Cheese p.74, 40	Herb-Crusted Rack of Lamb with Grilled Asparagus p. 87	Chia Raspberry Jam Filled Doughnut Holes p. 112
Day 26	Greek-Style Spinach and Olive Breakfast Muffins p.26	Stuffed Portobello Mushrooms with Ground Turkey & Feta Cheese p. 59	Coconut Shrimp with Avocado Dip p. 106	Lemon Blueberry Cake P. 111
Day 27	Pecan Pie Granola Bars p. 26	Mediterranean Lamb Kebabs with Tzatziki Sauce and Crispy Air-Fried Chickpea Salad p. 84, 35	Parmesan Crusted Organic Chicken Fillets p. 71	Low-Sugar Hazelnut Chocolate Truffles p. 113
Day 28	Zucchini and Feta Fritters p. 21	Pork Tenderloin with Fresh Herbs and Asparagus and Goat Cheese Salad p. 97, 34	Grilled Salmon Kale Salad with Lemon Dressing p. 30	Creamy Greek Yogurt Cheesecake with Mixed Berries p. 114
Day 29	Peanut Butter and Jelly Protein Bars p.22	Teriyaki Glazed Drumsticks with Roasted Pumpkin and Arugula Superfood Bowl p. 69, 32	Lamb Meatballs Stuffed with Feta Cheese in Tomato Sauce p. 88	Keto Avocado Brownies p. 114
Day 30	Coconut Flour Blueberry Muffins p.23	Sesame-Ginger Turkey Meatballs with Asian Style Broccoli Slaw with Crunchy Tofu p.63, 30	Chicken Bruschetta with Italian Baked Eggplant Sticks with Marinara Dip p. 40, 44	Cinnamon and Almond Biscotti p. 108

Recipe Index

A

Almond Flour
Low-Sugar Apple Fritters, 18
Zucchini and Carrot Morning Glory Muffins, 24
Cinnamon-Spiced Zucchini Bread Slices, 12
Almond Flour Cinnamon Muffins, 14
Berry Chia Seed Breakfast Bars, 19
Cauliflower Hash Browns, 20
Almond Flour Banana Bread Slices, 21
Zucchini and Feta Fritters, 21
Peanut Butter and Jelly Protein Bars, 22
Blueberry Lemon Scones, 25
Greek-Style Spinach and Olive Breakfast Muffins, 26
Low-Carb Caesar Salad with Air-Fried Shrimp, 29
Chicken Bruschetta, 40
Italian Baked Eggplant Sticks with Marinara Dip, 44
Chicken Meatball Italian Wedding Soup, 53
Parmesan Crusted Organic Chicken Fillets, 71
Cinnamon and Almond Biscotti, 108
Coconut and Blueberry Cheesecake Bites, 108
Almond Joy Keto Cookies, 110
Peanut Butter Banana Muffins, 110
Lemon Blueberry Cake, 111
Gluten-Free Strawberry Rhubarb Crumble, 112
Chia Raspberry Jam Filled Doughnut Holes, 112
Creamy Greek Yogurt Cheesecake with Mixed Berries, 114

Almond Milk
Greek-Style Spinach and Olive Breakfast Muffins, 26
Vegetable & Egg Muffins, 12
Low-Carb Breakfast Burritos, 15
Coconut Flour Pumpkin Pancakes, 16
Asparagus and Mushroom Scramble, 17
Low-Sugar Apple Fritters, 18
Vegetable and Cheese Frittata, 20
Almond Flour Banana Bread Slices, 21
Coconut Flour Blueberry Muffins, 23

Apple
Low-Sugar Apple Fritters, 18

Artichoke
Marinated Artichoke Heart and Shrimp Pasta-Salad, 31

Arugula
Roasted Pumpkin and Arugula Superfood Bowl, 32

Asparagus
Asparagus and Mushroom Scramble, 17
Asparagus and Goat Cheese Salad, 34
Lemon-Pepper Asparagus Spears, 39
Balsamic-Glazed Top Sirloin Steak and Asparagus Bundles, 80
Herb-Crusted Rack of Lamb with Grilled Asparagus, 87
Lean Bacon-Wrapped Asparagus Skewers, 98

Avocado
Smoked Salmon and Avocado Toast, 13
Avocado Egg Boats, 13
Southwest Black Bean and Sweet Potato Breakfast, 16 Bowl
Chickpea Avocado Toast, 19
Breakfast Burrito Bowl, 24
Grilled Salmon Kale Salad with Lemon Dressing, 30
Grilled Chicken and Avocado Salad, 33
Crispy Turkey Tacos with Avocado Crema, 56
Ground Beef Lettuce Wraps with Avocado Salsa, 79
Coconut Shrimp with Avocado Dip, 106
Keto Avocado Brownies, 114

B
Barley
Vegetable Barley Soup, 49

Beans

Southwest Black Bean and Sweet Potato Breakfast Bowl, 16

Breakfast Burrito Bowl, 24

Warm Salmon Niçoise Salad, 33

Spicy Sweet Potato and Black Bean Salad, 34

Air-Fried Green Beans Almondine, 39

Fresh Herbs and Lemon Green Beans, 45

Hearty Turkey and Bean Chili Soup, 52

Classic Minestrone Made Low-Carb, 53

Beetroot

Beetroot and Feta Salad, 37

Bell Pepper

Southwest Black Bean and Sweet Potato Breakfast, Bowl, 16

Stuffed Bell Peppers with Eggs and Turkey Sausage, 17

Breakfast Burrito Bowl, 24

Asian Style Broccoli Slaw with Crunchy Tofu, 30

Spicy Sweet Potato and Black Bean Salad, 34

Warm Mediterranean Vegetable Salad, 35

Sesame Ginger Broccoli Stir-fry, 43

Spicy Chicken & Veggie Soup with Tortilla Strips, 49

Greek Yogurt Marinated Chicken Skewers, 75

Vegetable & Egg Muffins, 12

Low-Carb Breakfast Burritos, 15

Protein-Packed Quinoa Breakfast Bowl, 15

Vegetable and Cheese Frittata, 20

Fresh Garden Vegetable Quinoa Bowl, 31

Italian Herb Roasted Bell Peppers, 43

Low-Carb Turkey Stuffed Bell Peppers, 55

Stuffed Bell Peppers with Ground Beef, 77

Greek Style Stuffed Bell Peppers with Ground Lamb, 86

Stuffed Bell Peppers with Ground Pork, 93

Cajun Shrimp Skewers with Grilled Bell Peppers, 103

Breakfast Pizza on Cauliflower Crust, 22

Breakfast Sweet Potato Boats, 25

Roasted Red Pepper Gazpacho, 50

Low-Carb Mexican Fiesta Stuffed Organic Chicken, Breast, 70

Broccoli

Asian Style Broccoli Slaw with Crunchy Tofu, 30

Sesame Ginger Broccoli Stir-fry, 43

Creamy Broccoli Soup with Air-Fryer Croutons, 48

Turkey & Vegetable Stir Fry, 55

Beef and Broccoli Stir-fry, 77

Herb-Crusted Haddock with Steamed Broccoli, 102

Lemon-infused Chicken Breast with Steamed Broccoli, 66

Sesame-Ginger Beef Stir-Fry, 81

Brussels Sprouts

Crispy Brussels Sprouts with Balsamic Glaze, 41

Garlic-Parmesan Air Fryer Brussels Sprouts, 46

Herb-Roasted Turkey Tenderloin with Roasted, Vegetables, 57

Balsamic Glazed Brussels Sprouts & Ground Turkey, 59

C
Calamari Rings

Mediterranean Stuffed Calamari Rings, 104

Catfish Fillets

Cajun Spiced Catfish with Sautéed Spinach, 102

Cauliflower

Cauliflower Hash Browns, 20

Breakfast Pizza on Cauliflower Crust, 22

Breakfast Burrito Bowl, 24

Cauliflower 'Mac' and Cheese, 40

Cauliflower Rice Pilaf with Carrots and Peas, 42

Cauliflower & Cheddar Cheese Soup, 50

Classic Minestrone Made Low-Carb, 53

Low-Carb Turkey Stuffed Bell Peppers, 55

Stuffed Bell Peppers with Ground Beef, 77

Shepherd's Pie with Cauliflower Mash, 85

Stuffed Bell Peppers with Ground Pork, 93

Cheddar Cheese

Cauliflower & Cheddar Cheese Soup, 50

Low-Carb Mexican Fiesta Stuffed Organic Chicken Breast, 70

Cheesy Spinach Air Fryer Omelette, 13

Low-Carb Breakfast Burritos, 15

Stuffed Bell Peppers with Eggs and Turkey Sausage, 17

Egg and Cheese Stuffed Tomatoes, 23

Cauliflower 'Mac' and Cheese, 40

Cherry Tomatoes

Protein-Packed Quinoa Breakfast Bowl, 15

Chickpea Avocado Toast, 19

Vegetable and Cheese Frittata, 20

Crunchy Greens Salad with Grilled Chicken and Herbs, 28

Mediterranean Tuna Salad with Fresh Herbs, 28
Marinated Artichoke Heart and Shrimp Pasta-Salad, 31
Grilled Chicken and Avocado Salad, 33
Warm Salmon Niçoise Salad, 33
Crispy Air-Fried Chickpea Salad, 35
Mediterranean Greek Salad with Grilled Chicken, 68
Chicken Bruschetta (No-Bread Version), 73
Warm Halloumi and Tomato Salad, 37

Chia Seeds
Berry Chia Seed Breakfast Bars, 19

Chicken Breast
Grilled Chicken and Avocado Salad, 33
Spicy Chicken & Veggie Soup with Tortilla Strips, 49
Chicken Zoodle Pro, 52
Chicken Satay with Peanut Sauce, 73
Greek Yogurt Marinated Chicken Skewers, 75
Crunchy Greens Salad with Grilled Chicken and Herbs, 28
Chicken Meatball Italian Wedding Soup, 53
Mediterranean Greek Salad with Grilled Chicken, 68
Parmesan Crusted Organic Chicken Fillets, 71
Chicken and Zucchini Meatballs, 74
Chicken Piccata with Capers, 72
Lemon-infused Chicken Breast with Steamed Broccoli, 66
Healthy Chicken Cordon Bleu, 67
Low-Carb Mexican Fiesta Stuffed Organic Chicken Breast, 70
Caprese Style Stuffed Grilled-Chicken, 71
BBQ Pulled Grilled-Chicken Lettuce Wraps, 72
Chicken Bruschetta (No-Bread Version), 73

Chicken Drumsticks
Savory Garlic & Herb Chicken Drumsticks, 66
Teriyaki Glazed Drumsticks, 69

Chicken Tenders

Chicken Tenders with Almond Flour Coating, 74

Chicken Thighs
Crispy Sesame Ginger Chicken Thighs, 68
Curry-Spiced Chicken Thighs, 75

Chicken Wings
Spicy Buffalo Chicken Wings with Celery Sticks, 67

Chickpea Flour
Chickpea Pancakes with Herbs, 18

Chickpea
Chickpea Avocado Toast, 19
Mediterranean Tuna Salad with Fresh Herbs, 28
Fresh Garden Vegetable Quinoa Bowl, 31
Crispy Air-Fried Chickpea Salad, 35
Mediterranean Spiced Air Fryer Chickpeas, 45

Coconut Flour
Coconut Flour Pumpkin Pancakes, 16
Low-Sugar Apple Fritters, 18
Coconut Flour Blueberry Muffins, 23
Zucchini and Carrot Morning Glory Muffins, 24
Blueberry Lemon Scones, 25
Greek-Style Spinach and Olive Breakfast Muffins, 26
Peanut Butter Banana Muffins, 110

Cod Fillets
Chili-Lime Cod Fish Tacos Wrapped in Lettuce, 101

E
Eggplant
Warm Mediterranean Vegetable Salad, 35
Italian Baked Eggplant Sticks with Marinara Dip, 44
Skillet-style Ground Lamb and Eggplant Moussaka, 87
Hearty Grilled Aubergine & Ground Beef Lasagna, 82

Egg
Cinnamon-Spiced Zucchini Bread Slices, 12
Cheesy Spinach Air Fryer Omelette, 13
Avocado Egg Boats, 13
Almond Flour Cinnamon Muffins, 14
Low-Carb Breakfast Burritos, 15
Protein-Packed Quinoa Breakfast Bowl, 15
Coconut Flour Pumpkin Pancakes, 16
Southwest Black Bean and Sweet Potato Breakfast Bowl, 16
Asparagus and Mushroom Scramble, 17
Stuffed Bell Peppers with Eggs and Turkey Sausage, 17
Low-Sugar Apple Fritters, 18
Berry Chia Seed Breakfast Bars, 19
Cauliflower Hash Browns, 20
Vegetable and Cheese Frittata, 20

Almond Flour Banana Bread Slices, 21
Zucchini and Feta Fritters, 21
Breakfast Pizza on Cauliflower Crust, 22
Peanut Butter and Jelly Protein Bars, 22
Coconut Flour Blueberry Muffins, 23
Egg and Cheese Stuffed Tomatoes, 23
Zucchini and Carrot Morning Glory Muffins, 24
Breakfast Burrito Bowl, 24
Blueberry Lemon Scones, 25
Breakfast Sweet Potato Boats, 25
Warm Salmon Niçoise Salad, 33
Chicken Tenders with Almond Flour Coating, 74

F
Feta Cheese
Vegetable and Cheese Frittata, 20
Beetroot and Feta Salad, 37
Greek Style Stuffed Bell Peppers with Ground Lamb, 86
Lamb Meatballs Stuffed with Feta Cheese in Tomato Sauce, 88
Avocado Egg Boats, 13
Protein-Packed Quinoa Breakfast Bowl, 15
Zucchini and Feta Fritters, 21
Breakfast Sweet Potato Boats, 25
Greek-Style Spinach and Olive Breakfast Muffins, 26
Stuffed Portobello Mushrooms with Ground Turkey & Feta Cheese, 59
Greek-Style Turkey Burgers with Tzatziki, 64
Mediterranean Greek Salad with Grilled Chicken, 68

G
Goat Cheese
Asparagus and Goat Cheese Salad, 34
Warm Mushroom and Spinach Salad, 36

Ground Turkey
Hearty Turkey and Bean Chili Soup, 52
Low-Carb Turkey Stuffed Bell Peppers, 55
Crispy Turkey Tacos with Avocado Crema, 56
Spicy Ground Turkey Lettuce Wraps, 57
Turkey Meatball Soup with Spiralized Veggies, 58
Balsamic Glazed Brussels Sprouts & Ground Turkey, 59
Stuffed Portobello Mushrooms with Ground Turkey & Feta Cheese, 59
Turkey Zucchini Boats with Mozzarella Topping, 60
Low-Carb BBQ Basted Mini-Turkey Meatloaves, 61
Asian-Inspired Sesame-Ginger Ground Turkey Wraps, 61
Sesame-Ginger Turkey Meatballs, 63
Greek-Style Turkey Burgers with Tzatziki, 64

H
Haddock Fillets
Herb-Crusted Haddock with Steamed Broccoli, 102

Halibut Steak
Fragrant Halibut Steaks with Citrus Vinaigrette, 105

Halloumi Cheese
Warm Halloumi and Tomato Salad, 37

K
Kale
Grilled Salmon Kale Salad with Lemon Dressing, 30

L
Lamb Loin
Rosemary and Thyme-Infused Lamb Chops, 84

Lean Beef
Beef and Broccoli Stir-fry, 77

Lean Ground Beef
Stuffed Bell Peppers with Ground Beef, 77
Ground Beef Lettuce Wraps with Avocado Salsa, 79
Homemade Beef Meatballs, 80
Cheesy Stuffed Mushrooms with Minced Beef, 82
Hearty Grilled Aubergine & Ground Beef Lasagna, 82

Lean Ground Lamb
Shepherd's Pie with Cauliflower Mash, 85
Greek Style Stuffed Bell Peppers with Ground Lamb, 86
Skillet-style Ground Lamb and Eggplant Moussaka, 87
Lamb Meatballs Stuffed with Feta Cheese in Tomato Sauce, 88
Spinach & Minced Lamb Stuffed Zucchini Boats, 89
Middle Eastern Kofta Wraps, 89

Lean Ground Pork
Stuffed Bell Peppers with Ground Pork, 93
Spicy Ground Pork Stuffed Mushroom Caps, 97

Lean Lamb
Mediterranean Lamb Kebabs with Tzatziki Sauce, 84
Cumin Spiced Lamb Skewers with Grilled Veggies, 85

M
Mozzarella Cheese
Caprese Style Stuffed Grilled-Chicken, 71
Hearty Grilled Aubergine & Ground Beef Lasagna, 82
Breakfast Pizza on Cauliflower Crust, 22
Turkey Zucchini Boats with Mozzarella Topping, 60

Mushrooms
Spicy Ground Pork Stuffed Mushroom Caps, 97
Mushroom caps stuffed with clams, 106
Asparagus and Mushroom Scramble, 17
Breakfast Pizza on Cauliflower Crust, 22
Warm Mushroom and Spinach Salad, 36
Stuffed Mushroom Caps with Spinach and Ricotta, 46
Creamy Mushroom Soup with Thyme, 51
Stuffed Portobello Mushrooms with Ground Turkey & Feta Cheese, 59
Hearty Air-Fried Turkey Sausage Casserole, 62
Cheesy Stuffed Mushrooms with Minced Beef, 82

O
Okra
Spicy Okra with Cool Yogurt Dip, 41

P
Parmesan Cheese
Asparagus and Mushroom Scramble, 17
Cauliflower Hash Browns, 20
Breakfast Pizza on Cauliflower Crust, 22
Egg and Cheese Stuffed Tomatoes, 23
Low-Carb Caesar Salad with Air-Fried Shrimp, 29
Cauliflower 'Mac' and Cheese, 40
Chicken Bruschetta, 40
Italian Baked Eggplant Sticks with Marinara Dip, 44
Stuffed Mushroom Caps with Spinach and Ricotta, 46
Garlic-Parmesan Air Fryer Brussels Sprouts, 46
Parmesan-Crusted Turkey Tenders, 62
Parmesan Crusted Organic Chicken Fillets, 71
Homemade Beef Meatballs, 80
Parmesan Crusted Pork Chops, 92

Pork Tenderloin
Garlic and Herb Pork Tenderloin, 92
Apple Cider Marinated Lean Pulled-Pork Wraps, 96
Pork Tenderloin with Fresh Herbs, 97
Sweet & Sour Pulled-Pork Lettuce Wraps, 98

Pumpkin
Coconut Flour Pumpkin Pancakes, 16
Roasted Pumpkin and Arugula Superfood Bowl, 32
Roasted Pumpkin Bisque with Greek Yogurt Swirl, 50

Q
Quinoa
Protein-Packed Quinoa Breakfast Bowl, 15
Fresh Garden Vegetable Quinoa Bowl, 31
Roasted Pumpkin and Arugula Superfood Bowl, 32

S
Salmon
Smoked Salmon and Avocado Toast, 13
Grilled Salmon Kale Salad with Lemon Dressing, 30
Warm Salmon Niçoise Salad, 33
Zesty Lemon Garlic Air-Fried Salmon Fillets, 100
Asian-Style Sesame Ginger Salmon Patties, 104

Sea Scallops
Lemon Pepper Scallops, 103

Shrimps
Low-Carb Caesar Salad with Air-Fried Shrimp, 29
Marinated Artichoke Heart and Shrimp Pasta-Salad, 31
Shrimp Scampi with Zucchini Noodles, 100
Cajun Shrimp Skewers with Grilled Bell Peppers, 103
Coconut Shrimp with Avocado Dip, 106

Spinach
Vegetable & Egg Muffins, 12
Cheesy Spinach Air Fryer Omelette, 13
Low-Carb Breakfast Burritos, 15
Stuffed Bell Peppers with Eggs and Turkey Sausage, 17
Vegetable and Cheese Frittata, 20
Breakfast Sweet Potato Boats, 25
Greek-Style Spinach and Olive Breakfast Muffins, 26
Spinach & Strawberry Salad with Balsamic Vinaigrette, 29

Marinated Artichoke Heart and Shrimp Pasta-Salad, 31
Summer Berry Almond Spinach Salad, 32
Warm Mushroom and Spinach Salad, 36
Stuffed Mushroom Caps with Spinach and Ricotta, 46
Stuffed Portobello Mushrooms with Ground Turkey & Feta Cheese, 59
Spinach & Minced Lamb Stuffed Zucchini Boats, 89
Cajun Spiced Catfish with Sautéed Spinach, 102

Sweet Potato
Southwest Black Bean and Sweet Potato Breakfast Bowl, 16
Breakfast Sweet Potato Boats, 25
Spicy Sweet Potato and Black Bean Salad, 34

T
Tilapia Fillets
Spicy Panko Crusted Tilapia Filets, 105

Tofu
Asian Style Broccoli Slaw with Crunchy Tofu, 30

Tuna
Mediterranean Tuna Salad with Fresh Herbs, 28
Teriyaki Glazed Tuna Steaks, 101

Turkey Breast
Turkey & Vegetable Stir Fry, 55
Zesty Lemon-Garlic Air-Fried Turkey Breast, 56
Thanksgiving-Style Sliced Turkey Breast, 60
Teriyaki Turkey Skewers with Pineapple, 64
Parmesan-Crusted Turkey Tenders, 62

Turkey Drumsticks
Buffalo-Style Turkey Drumsticks, 63

Turkey Legs
Rosemary & Garlic Infused Turkey Legs, 58

Turkey Sausage
Stuffed Bell Peppers with Eggs and Turkey Sausage, 17
Hearty Air-Fried Turkey Sausage Casserole, 62

Turkey Tenderloin
Herb-Roasted Turkey Tenderloin with Roasted Vegetables, 57
Garlic & Rosemary Roasted Turnips, 42

W
Walnut
Almond Flour Cinnamon Muffins, 14
Almond Flour Banana Bread Slices, 21
Asparagus and Goat Cheese Salad, 34
Warm Mushroom and Spinach Salad, 36
Coconut Flour Blueberry Muffins, 23

Z
Zucchini
Cinnamon-Spiced Zucchini Bread Slices, 12
Protein-Packed Quinoa Breakfast Bowl, 15
Zucchini and Feta Fritters, 21
Fresh Garden Vegetable Quinoa Bowl, 31
Warm Mediterranean Vegetable Salad, 35
Chicken Bruschetta, 40
Spicy Chicken & Veggie Soup with Tortilla Strips, 49
Vegetable Barley Soup, 49
Roasted Red Pepper Gazpacho, 50
Chicken Zoodle Pro, 52
Classic Minestrone Made Low-Carb, 53
Herb-Roasted Turkey Tenderloin with Roasted, Vegetables, 57
Turkey Zucchini Boats with Mozzarella Topping, 60
Hearty Air-Fried Turkey Sausage Casserole, 62
Chicken and Zucchini Meatballs, 74
Greek Yogurt Marinated Chicken Skewers, 75
Mediterranean Lamb Kebabs with Tzatziki Sauce, 84
Cumin Spiced Lamb Skewers with Grilled Veggies, 85
Spinach & Minced Lamb Stuffed Zucchini Boats, 89
Lean Pork Skewers with Lemon Zest, 93
Shrimp Scampi with Zucchini Noodles, 100
Zucchini and Carrot Morning Glory Muffins, 24

Printed in Great Britain
by Amazon